REFORMING PHILADELPHIA,

1682–2022

RICHARDSON DILWORTH

TEMPLE UNIVERSITY PRESS
Philadelphia • Rome • Tokyo

TEMPLE UNIVERSITY PRESS
Philadelphia, Pennsylvania 19122
tupress.temple.edu

Library of Congress Cataloging-in-Publication Data

Names: Dilworth, Richardson, 1971– author.
Title: Reforming Philadelphia, 1682–2022 / Richardson Dilworth.
Other titles: Political lessons from American cities.
Description: Philadelphia : Temple University Press, 2023. | Series:
   Political lessons from American cities | Includes bibliographical
   references and index. | Summary: "Uses Philadelphia as a case study to
   argue that political reform is a constant though not always dominant
   theme in city politics, maintained through various interconnected social
   and professional networks"— Provided by publisher.
Identifiers: LCCN 2022025019 (print) | LCCN 2022025020 (ebook) | ISBN
   9781439920060 (cloth) | ISBN 9781439920077 (paperback) | ISBN
   9781439920084 (pdf)
Subjects: LCSH: Municipal government—Pennsylvania—Philadelphia—Case
   studies. | Political culture—Pennsylvania—Philadelphia. | Urban
   policy—Pennsylvania—Philadelphia. | Philadelphia (Pa.)—Politics and
   government.
Classification: LCC JS1265 .D55 2023 (print) | LCC JS1265 (ebook) | DDC
   342/.0974811—dc23/eng/20220816
LC record available at https://lccn.loc.gov/2022025019
LC ebook record available at https://lccn.loc.gov/2022025020

∞ The paper used in this publication meets the requirements of the American National
Standard for Information Sciences—Permanence of Paper for Printed Library Materials,
ANSI Z39.48-1992

Printed in the United States of America

9 8 7 6 5 4 3 2 1

REFORMING PHILADELPHIA, 1682–2022

In the series *Political Lessons from American Cities*,
edited by RICHARDSON DILWORTH

·

ALSO IN THIS SERIES:

Ann O'M. Bowman, *Reinventing the Austin City Council*

To Sam

CONTENTS

ACKNOWLEDGMENTS

I owe a great debt of gratitude to Aaron Javsicas, editor-in-chief at Temple University Press, and the support he has shown for this book and the larger series of which it is a part—though it is certainly worth mentioning that the idea for the series began with a conversation between myself and Suzanne Flinchbaugh when she was at Johns Hopkins University Press. My book also benefited from the feedback of several kind and smart folks, most notably Dave Marshall from the Friends Select School, Dave Davies from WHYY, Jeff Hornstein from the Economy League, my wife Martha Lucy, and two anonymous academic reviewers—later revealed to be my academic idols Jon Teaford and Jessica Trounstine—who provided excellent feedback on my original proposal and who both returned five years later to comment on the full manuscript. Special thanks to Jack Santucci for making the graph in Figure I.1. Thanks as well to Larry Platt, Jon Geeting, Alison Perelman, Therese Madden, and John Kromer; and to Dan Shepalevy and Roxanne Patel Shepalevy, who, over a campfire, steered me gently away from my original title idea ("Reform Cycles in Philadelphia Politics"), suggesting it sounded too much like a book about a washing machine. Finally, thanks to all Philadelphia journalists past and present who have written about the city's politics, whom I have relied on heavily in writing this book, as my endnotes indicate.

This book is dedicated to my son, Sam, who has endured a decade of life in Philadelphia through no choice of his own.

REFORMING PHILADELPHIA,
1682–2022

INTRODUCTION

Reform Cycles and
Urban Political Development

This book presents a political history of Philadelphia explained in terms of *reform cycles,* or periods when new conceptions of the city and its purpose in the world inspired people to try to change the city government. These reformers have sometimes portrayed themselves as fighting against a corrupt "machine" of politicians using the city government simply to enrich themselves. As a remedy, political scientists at the turn of the twentieth century recommended such things as civil service, city managers, and smaller city councils. These reforms did not cure corruption but were widely adopted.

After World War II, political scientists stopped making so many recommendations and began studying cities as microcosms of how power functioned in society; by the 1970s, this "community power" discussion was dissipating, cities were mired in an "urban crisis," and the academic literature fragmented into discussions of ungovernable cities, race and class conflict, and cities' dependence on the larger political and economic system.[1] By the 1980s and 1990s, much of the urban politics literature focused on how business and government cooperated to create "regimes" or "growth machines."[2] Most recently, urbanist political scientists have returned both to issues of racial and economic inequality and to local parties and elections.[3]

In short, every generation of scholars has understood cities differently and thus developed new conceptual models to explain city politics. One result is a deficit in explanations of city politics across time—that is, *urban political development.* My goal, then, is to use one model to explain Philadelphia politics over its 340-year existence. To do so, I borrow the Progressive Era term *reform* and expand it to describe a cyclical process that might also explain Philadelphia politics in the 1850s, 1880s, 1950s, 1990s, and 2010s. In my expanded usage, a reform cycle includes all or most of the following:

1. A new idea regarding the city and its purpose in the world
2. Actors who attempt to take control of city government and reform it in the image of this new idea
3. Actors conceived of as thwarting reform (the "machine")
4. Elections in which reformers gain some control over city government
5. The implementation of ideas that transform the city to some degree
6. Public recognition, typically provided through the press, that reform occurred

There is a necessary tension between imposing the same conceptual framework (reform cycles) on different eras of Philadelphia politics and providing enough detail so that each era appears relatively unique. This is part of the nature of case-based research, and each reform cycle I identify should be understood in social scientific terms as a case study. All case studies are necessarily selective and subjective interpretations of events; what validates them is a qualitative and historical version of the scientific standard of replicability, namely, the extent to which readers agree with my interpretations even when I have provided enough detail for alternate explanations.

My reform cycles model borrows from at least three well-known political science models: Electoral realignments, the "multiple streams" approach, and punctuated equilibria. Electoral realignments occur when new issues cut across existing party cleavages. As parties respond to these issues they gain new adherents but alienate others, leading to broad shifts in electoral behavior that usher in new party systems, which most textbooks demarcate by the "critical elections" of 1828, 1860, 1896, 1932, and 1968.[4] Similar to the realignment model, my conception of reform is cyclical, and the cycles in Philadelphia often mirrored national realignments, such as Philadelphians' shift to Republicans in the 1850s and 1860s and to Democrats in the 1950s—the latter described by political scientist James Sundquist as an "aftershock" of the national realignment in the 1930s.[5] More generally, practically every reform cycle I identify herein is in some way connected to national politics but the nature of that connection has changed over time: While earlier reform cycles tended to reflect national party realignments, more recently, specific Democratic presidential candidates—most notably Howard Dean in 2004 and Bernie Sanders in 2016—have catalyzed local political coalitions that survive past the presidential campaigns and provide much of the momentum for local reform.

Key to my argument is that reform cycles depend on a continuous line of interrelated, reform-oriented organizations, stretching from the Board of Trade (BoT) in the 1840s to contemporary organizations such as Reclaim Philadelphia (Reclaim) and Philadelphia 3.0 (3.0), that have provided a steady stream of proposals and criticisms, forming what John Kingdon (the originator of the multiple streams approach) called the "policy primeval soup" from which the separate "streams" of problems, policies, and politics draw. These streams cross one another in largely random and unforeseeable moments that provide windows of opportunity for significant policy changes.[6]

Realignment theory defines regular cycles while the multiple streams approach emphasizes randomness and contingency, yet both frameworks assume stable institutions such as elections and party systems. Looking at one city over a long stretch of time provides an opportunity for examining how such institutions emerged and how the shapes they took affected the city's political development. Significant institutional changes that disrupt status quos are often described as "punctuated equilibria":[7] the classic example in Philadelphia being the period between 1838, the expansion in suffrage, and 1854, when state law transformed Philadelphia from a 2-square-mile city into a 130-square-mile consolidated city-county.

The 1854 consolidation was part of a reform cycle in which one set of elites, organized primarily through the BoT, reimagined the structure and functions of the city. It also provided the institutional basis for a new form of politics by creating the wards that still serve as the basis for the city's party system, which was also transformed by expanded suffrage. It is also worth noting that Philadelphia's political transformation in one fell swoop in 1854 distinguishes it from cities such as Boston, where territorial annexations were piecemeal and smaller in scope.

The winning vote percentage in the general election for Philadelphia mayor from 1839 to 2019 is provided in Figure I.1, which suggests that the 1854 consolidation stabilized what had previously been wildly fluctuating election results. Mayoral elections became reasonably competitive—Republicans won eight out of thirteen elections between 1854 and 1887—until a strong Republican machine took control, after which the party won mayoral elections by landslides from 1891 to 1932, with the notable exceptions of 1907 and 1911.

Chapter 1 addresses Philadelphia's development from 1682 up to the reform cycle that culminated in the 1854 consolidation; a new reform movement that emerged in the 1870s, resulting in Samuel King's election as mayor in 1881 and a new city charter in 1885; and the Republican machine that

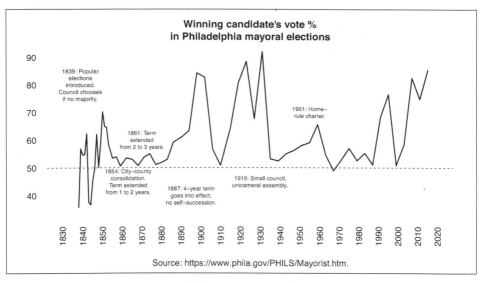

**Winning candidate's vote %
in Philadelphia mayoral elections**

1839: Popular elections introduced. Council chooses if no majority.

1861: Term extended from 2 to 3 years.

1951: Home-rule charter.

1854: City–county consolidation. Term extended from 1 to 2 years.

1887: 4–year term goes into effect; no self–succession.

1919: Small council, unicameral assembly.

Source: https://www.phila.gov/PHILS/Mayorlst.htm.

Figure I.1 The percentage of the vote received by the winning candidate for mayor, 1839–2019. The percentage of the winning vote could fall below 50 percent with more than two candidates running. (Graph by Jack Santucci. Data from the Department of Records, City of Philadelphia, available at www.phila.gov /PHILS/Mayorlst.htm. Accessed April 13, 2020.)

emerged in the 1880s and 1890s. Chapter 2 covers three twentieth-century reform cycles, starting with the mayoral elections of 1907, when incumbent John Weaver broke with the Republican Organization (sometimes simply known as the "Organization"), and of 1911, when reformer Rudolph Blankenburg was elected mayor.

Republicans continued to win elections in the 1930s but by significantly smaller margins. Democrats, strengthened by federal patronage and new leadership, allied with reform organizations after World War II, culminating in a new reform cycle with the adoption of a new charter and the election to mayor of Democratic reformers Joseph Clark in 1951 and Richardson Dilworth in 1955 and 1959.* By most accounts, this reform cycle concluded in 1962 when Dilworth resigned to run unsuccessfully for governor and was succeeded by city council president James Tate.

The 1950s also began the period of dramatic racial transition as Black people moved to Philadelphia in large numbers and white people left. De-

---

* Mayor Richardson Dilworth was my grandfather and namesake. He died when I was three years old, but my relation to him likely informs whatever unconscious biases I have when discussing Philadelphia politics.

spite Democrats' continued dominance, issues surrounding race, crime, and economic decline provided for more competitive elections, reminiscent of the 1860s and 1870s. Narrower mayoral victories stretched from Tate's first election in 1963 to Wilson Goode's victory over Frank Rizzo in 1987. Democratic reformers' early embrace of civil rights, in the 1950s, allowed for biracial political coalitions, and civil rights groups formed part of the broader reform movement though they also acted independently; Black politicians ran significant third-party mayoral campaigns in 1967, 1975, and 1979 (which, in part, explains the lower victory margins during these decades), and specifically Black reform groups such as the Black Political Forum (BPF) emerged.

Reform cycles are, in part, socially constructed products of collective memory, reflected most obviously in press coverage. And, in Philadelphia, Black politicians had less initial success defining themselves as reformers. Mayor Goode, for instance, was a classic good-government technocrat and self-identified reformer who does not fit into the historical narrative as such, partly because of some notable policy blunders but also because local media discussed him more in terms of race rather than reform. By contrast, the white mayor elected in 1991 after Goode, Edward Rendell, defined the next reform cycle. Rendell is not remembered as a reformer and did not define himself as such, but his mayoralty represents a reform cycle for several reasons. First, Rendell's election was simultaneous to the election of a new Democratic president who ushered in a new technocratic reformist dialogue about "reinventing government" as opposed to the previous Republican administrations during Goode's mayoralty that emphasized the idea, as Reagan put it, that "government is the problem." Second, Rendell offered a new vision of Philadelphia focused on downtown entertainment and nightlife and a new vision of city government through his embrace of the reinventing government movement. Third, Rendell took a vocally combative stance against municipal unions that had in the 1970s emerged as a new form of political machine. And, fourth, he was widely hailed as having saved the city from near bankruptcy, which was itself often blamed on Goode.[8]

In Chapter 3, I cover twenty-first century Philadelphia politics through the mayoralties of John Street, Michael Nutter, and the current mayor Jim Kenney. Street's narrow electoral victories are reminiscent of those from the 1960s and 1970s, while Nutter and Kenney's vote margins are more reminiscent of the period of Republican dominance in the 1890s and 1920s. Indeed, Street shared many similarities to Tate; both had been council presidents and were viewed as uncharismatic machine-oriented politicians who could not connect with upper-income white liberal reform voters. By contrast, Nutter was a classic good-government reformer who also presented a new image of a potentially "green" and "sustainable" city and who benefited from a local economic resurgence only momentarily halted by the Great Recession.

Yet, by the time of Nutter's mayoralty, there were evident contradictions out of which a new politics emerged. Despite its economic resurgence, Philadelphia maintains a persistently high rate of poverty, and the Democratic "machine" is a weak federation of fluctuating political coalitions, yet, overwhelmingly, liberal Democratic voters elect Democrats by margins of victory reminiscent of the Republican Organization's heyday. In a deeply unequal city with a liberal electorate, a new progressive coalition has found fertile ground, seeded by activism generated both by Bernie Sanders's 2016 presidential campaign and in reaction to Donald Trump's election. Even earlier, Kenney won the 2015 Democratic mayoral primary by tacking leftward, as had successful mayoral candidates in other cities in 2013. I thus conclude Chapter 3 by speculating on the future of Philadelphia politics, in a city marked by a vibrant and electorally successful progressive movement, still experiencing an economic resurgence yet marked by deep inequalities, low voter turnout, and a fragmented and weakened press. Readers who make it that far can then turn to my even more irresponsible speculations in the Conclusion regarding reform cycles and urban history.

CONSTRUCTING THE CONTEXT
FOR REFORM

T he reform cycles that characterized Philadelphia politics in the twentieth and twenty-first centuries were structured by the institutional
framework that emerged from the city's founding in 1682—planned
as the "great towne" of William Penn's land grant, Pennsylvania—into the
establishment in the late nineteenth century of a "machine-reform" style of
urban politics. The city's uniquely diverse economy produced a set of inter-
locking and elite civic, social, and professional societies and associations
that served as the institutional framework from which successive reform
movements were launched. An incipient reform network was the force behind municipal stock subscriptions to the Pennsylvania Railroad (PRR) in
1846 and the 1854 city-county consolidation. Yet, city-county consolidation
also provided the institutional basis for a Republican political machine after
the Civil War.

The Republican machine motivated business elites to form successive
reform-oriented societies and associations in the 1870s and 1880s, relying
largely on the membership of older organizations such as the Board of Trade
(BoT) and Union League. These groups served as the organizational spring-
boards for the first full-fledged reform cycle in the 1880s, which included a
brief alliance between reform Republicans and the Democratic Party, the
election of reform Democrats to the citywide offices of controller and mayor,
and passage of a new city charter—the "Bullitt Charter"—by the state legislature in 1885. Ironically, the Bullitt Charter helped consolidate the statewide
Republican Party machine in the 1890s. And, while the reform organizations

of the 1870s and 1880s had largely disappeared by the 1890s, they also served as the bases for establishing new organizations and a new reform cycle in the 1900s and 1910s, discussed in Chapter 2.

The City in the Beginning

Philadelphia was planned as a street grid of approximately two square miles between the Schuylkill and the Delaware Rivers. Though founded later than New York City, Boston, Newport, and Charleston, Philadelphia was, by 1690, second in size only to Boston. And, while Boston's population stagnated in the mid-eighteenth century, Philadelphia continued to grow. Early development clustered along the Delaware River, spilling beyond the original grid and extending into what became the municipalities of Northern Liberties and Southwark, to the north and south of the city, respectively. By the first U.S. Census in 1790, Philadelphia, Northern Liberties, and Southwark ranked as the second, sixth, and tenth largest cities in the country, respectively, with a combined population of 48,705, making it a much larger urban center than New York City, which, in the same year, had a population of 33,131 (and over a larger territory, as New York included all of Manhattan Island). Thus, Philadelphia in the eighteenth century is typically referred to as the second largest city in the British Empire, smaller only than London.[1] (See Figure 1.1.)

Philadelphia's dramatic early growth was, in part, a function of its role as the primary incubator for the colonies' medical, scientific, financial, banking, and insurance industries. The city was home to the first North American medical school (founded in 1765 at the University of Pennsylvania), hospital (Pennsylvania Hospital, founded 1751), and stock exchange (London Coffee House, founded 1754) and the second fire insurance company (the Philadelphia Contributionship, founded 1752, seventeen years after a short-lived company in Charleston). There were numerous other unique scientific, philosophical, and industrial societies, not a few of which were the brainchild of Benjamin Franklin, who was certainly an exceptional individual but also a reflection of the city's culture of innovation.[2]

Part of the explanation for Philadelphia's precociousness was the dominant Quaker influence that encouraged egalitarianism, antiauthoritarianism, and tolerance—especially important for the emergent medical profession, viewed with deep suspicion elsewhere in the colonies. Sociologist Digby Baltzell famously argued that Quaker egalitarianism and antiauthoritarianism also made the city and colony largely ungovernable. Indeed, Penn established a remarkably democratic but also unworkable "frame of government" for the colony that was revised three times between 1682 and 1701. Colonial assemblies were characterized by factional feuding and struggles.

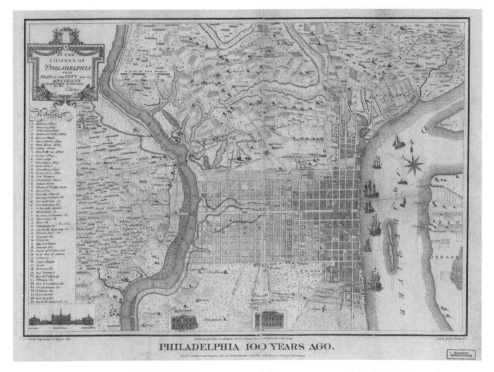

Figure 1.1 Map of Philadelphia as it would have appeared in 1775. Note the relative lack of development in the western part of the original street plan and the extension of the street plan north and south along the Delaware River into the municipalities of Northern Liberties and Southwark. (P. C. Varte and John Carbutt, *Philadelphia 100 Years Ago* [Philadelphia, 1875]. Map. Library of Congress, Geography and Map Division.)

Penn, who was in Pennsylvania for a total of only four years (1682–1684 and 1699–1701), appointed six separate deputy governors in the first decade of the colony's existence.[3]

As Baltzell put it, the Quakers "cared little about law and order in government as long as they were allowed to seek their fortunes in a laissez-faire and private way." The colony's earlier settlers were engaged in a wide variety of crafts and trades, and the city was surrounded by a region rich in fertile farmland and natural resources, most notably iron ore and coal. Its location near the base of the Delaware River meant that merchants traded with relative ease along the East Coast, into the Caribbean, and across the Atlantic.[4]

Combined with these locational advantages, Philadelphia's merchants built innovative financial institutions, starting with ground rents (available only in Maryland, Pennsylvania, and Delaware) by which properties could be purchased with relatively small sums but the new buyer was then subject to a perpetual interest rate. For buyers, ground rents made property owner-ship possible where it was otherwise prohibitively expensive, and, for sellers, the perpetual interest provided a stable source of investment income on the basis of which other financial institutions, such as savings banks and insurance companies, could be established.[5]

Merchants were most directly affected by the Crown's fiscal policies and thus a mercantile center such as Philadelphia played a lead role in the rebellion and revolution. The London Coffee House became the "unofficial head-quarters of rebellion. It hosted meetings of the city's Committee on Safety, as well as spontaneous riots and burnings of the Stamp Act."[6] The city served as the location for the first and second continental congresses, the Constitutional Convention of 1787, the national capital from 1791 to 1800, and the capital of Pennsylvania from 1735 to 1799. Given the extent of financial talent in the city, it was also no surprise that the city served as the home for the country's first three central banks (Bank of North America, Bank of the United States, and Second Bank of the United States) and the U.S. Mint.

At the turn of the nineteenth century, Philadelphia was an extensive but compact city. The mint, located less than a mile from the Delaware River, was at the "industrial outskirts of the city,"[7] while other major financial institutions were concentrated around Second, Third, and Chestnut Streets—the "Wall Street" of the eighteenth and early nineteenth centuries. (See Figure 1.2.) The growing working-class population lived in suburbs such as Northern Liberties and Southwark and the western part of the city while more affluent families lived in the center, though many of the "lower sort . . . continued to inhabit the center city region, crowding primarily into cheap shelter in alleys, courts, and lanes and leaving the major thoroughfares to the middling and better sort of citizens."[8]

The city itself, first granted a charter by Penn in 1691, was run by elites as a sort of private business club—or, as one historian put it, "an incestuous association dominated by members of a relatively few wealthy families."[9] The city officers, "invariably chosen from the mercantile class,"[10] were a mayor, recorder, six aldermen, and twelve common council members all appointed for life except for the mayor, who was elected annually from among, and by, the aldermen.[11] As was typical of early American municipal corporations, Philadelphia's officers focused mostly on regulating trade and the public markets and expended very little on what would today be understood as public services. Such things as night watchmen and a street paving program were established (in 1751 and 1762, respectively) not by the city but by independent commissions established by the colonial assembly.[12] In poorer areas, "streets generally went unpaved, watchmen made rounds sporadically, scavengers

Figure 1.2 The financial district of Philadelphia in the late 1700s: Second and Chestnut Streets, facing Christ Church. (From John F. Watson, *Annals of Philadelphia, and Pennsylvania, in the Olden Time* [Philadelphia: J. M. Stoddart, 1879], 195.)

appeared infrequently, and mounds of garbage fed a multitude of pigs, chickens, dogs, rats, and vermin."[13]

With the American Revolution came calls to democratize the city corporation, and, during the 1790s, there were reforms such as expanding voting rights and separating powers among the executive, legislative, and judicial branches. Inspired in part by the devastating 1793 yellow fever epidemic, the city focused more on public services such as street cleaning and water service. Philadelphia was, in fact, the first American city to establish a municipal waterworks, operational by 1801.[14]

In the same year Philadelphia gained a municipal waterworks, it lost the national capital to the marshlands of the District of Columbia and, along with that, the U.S. Department of the Treasury. The Bank of the United States headquarters stayed in the city until Congress revoked its charter in 1811, though the Second Bank, chartered by Congress in 1816, was also headquartered in Philadelphia. Thus, the city maintained its primacy as a financial capital but was losing some of its competitive advantages to New York City and Baltimore. New York Bay provided a superior port to the Delaware, especially after the Erie Canal, completed in 1825, created a new route for western trade. As ships became larger and could handle more cargo, most shipments from across the Atlantic came to New York and were then shipped to other eastern ports. Baltimore also had easier western access, most notably to the fertile and resource-rich Susquehanna Valley, while transport from Philadelphia was thwarted by the Allegheny Mountains.

The Manufacturing City

A diversified economy and an abundance of iron and coal in surrounding territories served as the basis for Philadelphia's growth as a manufacturing center. As economic historian Diane Lindstrom noted, "By 1840, Philadelphia's economy rested upon the twin pillars of commerce and manufacturing. . . . But commerce's contribution was on the wane, as foreign trade stagnated. Continued expansion of manufacturing rescued the city from the fate of lesser port towns such as Salem." Especially notable was Philadelphia's prominence in the production of textiles, machinery, tools, chemicals, "precious metals, drugs, and medicines . . . ," reflecting the city's role as a center of medical and scientific expertise.[15] Indeed, in the 1840s alone, five new medical schools were established in the city, though only two of these survived past the Civil War (the Homeopathic Medical College of Philadelphia and the Female Medical College of Pennsylvania, which merged in the late twentieth century and later became the Drexel University College of Medicine).[16]

Characterized by numerous small to midsize firms, Philadelphia's manufacturing sector was uniquely flexible and capable of innovation.[17] Given the numerous proprietorships in the city, there was ample membership for the BoT, founded in 1833 with 220 members and open to all types of businesses. The BoT eclipsed the Chamber of Commerce (established in 1801 and open only to maritime businesses), which it absorbed in 1845, and by 1869 it had 1,433 members.[18] The BoT was also a reflection of the larger trend of club formation in the mid-nineteenth century: "*Par excellence* the era of the urban parish church, the lodge, the benefit association, the social and athletic club, the political club, the fire company, and the gang. Over the whole range of sociability from the parties of the wealthy to the meanest boy's gang all Philadelphians sought a sense of social place and community in club life."[19] The volunteer fire companies also served as political clubs from which many young men established themselves as local ward leaders.

The city's growth as a manufacturing center was fueled by a large and growing working-class population. During the 1840s, Philadelphia County (the 130-square-mile territory in which Philadelphia city was located) grew at its fastest pace, increasing from 258,037 to 408,762 people between 1840 and 1850, with growth concentrated in the municipalities surrounding the central city, five of which ranked among the thirty largest cities in the country by 1850: Spring Garden (population 58,894), Northern Liberties (47,223), Kensington (46,774), Southwark (38,799), and Moyamensing (26,979).

The Workingmen's Party, active in the 1820s and 1830s, was instrumental in getting the state legislature to pass reforms such as free public schools, elimination of debtors' prison, and a ten-hour workday.[20] A new state constitution in 1838 expanded suffrage (though it also explicitly denied that right to Black people), which "meant that both the Whig and Democratic parties had to establish grassroots links in order to mobilize this new enlarged electorate at the polls, a task for which the career politician was ideally suited."[21]

The closing of the Second Bank in 1836 was followed by the financial panic of 1837, which was then followed by an economic depression into the mid-1840s,[22] which itself dovetailed with the arrival of Irish and mostly Catholic immigrants. The number of Irish arriving in Philadelphia was small compared to other cities but still significant enough to change the social composition of some neighborhoods, increasing anxieties about labor competition and fueling nativist, anti-Catholic resentment. The same was true for the city's free Black population (there were no slaves in the city by the mid-nineteenth century), which represented more than 10 percent of the population in 1840, the highest proportion of any major city besides Baltimore and New Orleans.

The increasing presence of abolitionists in the city fueled white fears and racial animosities. Increasingly violent episodes began in 1834, with violent attacks on Black people and their homes in the southern part of the city, spilling into Moyamensing. In 1838, a newly constructed abolitionist hall was burned to the ground by a mob of several thousand, and the following evening a smaller group attempted to burn down a Black orphanage. By the 1840s, as the number of Irish immigrants increased, Native American clubs proliferated. Riots that stemmed from efforts to enforce strikes transitioned into armed conflicts, leading to two periods of open warfare, in May and July 1844, in Kensington, Northern Liberties, and Southwark, between the nativists, Irish, sheriff, and state militia.[23]

City-County Consolidation and the Pennsylvania Railroad

The violence and collapse of public order in 1844 led at least some elites to propose the consolidation of Philadelphia County's twenty-nine municipalities into a single city, primarily to establish a professional and consolidated police force. A committee of political and economic elites drafted a consolidation bill and sent it to the legislature in Harrisburg, where it was ignored, possibly because another committee of even more formidable Philadelphia elites, mostly Whigs, were opposed, arguing that a consolidated city would be controlled by Democrats and would have to assume the larger municipal debts of the outlying districts. Another riot, in 1849, sparked renewed calls for consolidation, leading to the establishment of the "Marshal's Police" that covered multiple districts.[24]

In addition to riots, elites were increasingly concerned about the Baltimore and Ohio (B&O) railroad establishing a line to Pittsburgh, thereby providing Baltimore merchants with a western trading route that bypassed Philadelphia. Thomas Cope, a Philadelphia merchant, one of the BoT founders and its long-standing president, led the movement for a new rail line to connect Philadelphia to Pittsburgh that would also usurp the potential for a competing line to Baltimore. In 1846, the legislature approved, and the governor signed a charter for the PRR, stipulating that the corporation's commissioners had to raise "at least $3 million in stock subscriptions, with 10 percent paid in, and award construction contracts for a minimum of thirty miles of railroad" by July 30, 1847, or else the B&O would be granted the right to build a line to Pittsburgh.[25]

The PRR commissioners' expectations of raising the required money through private subscriptions were quickly dashed, and they instead turned to the Philadelphia city government to buy the bulk of the company's shares. The prospect of a massive municipal investment split elite Whigs into pro- and antisubscription factions for the 1846 council elections. The prosubscription forces won more seats, the city purchased $1.5 million worth of PRR stock, and the commissioners went about appointing a president and board of directors and planning an organizational structure for their new company.[26]

Through its role in the PRR stock subscription, the BoT leadership demonstrated a protoreformist, somewhat divisive, boosterish activism in the general direction of "progress." This was, as historian Albert Churella has noted, a specific subset of economic and social elites who, though they "had largely missed the opportunities associated with industrialization . . . still commanded considerable economic and social power. . . . They cared as deeply for Philadelphia's future as for their own commercial fortunes, and they were troubled at their city's rapid decline during the early decades of the nineteenth century from America's preeminent port to an also-ran."[27]

The PRR subscription created a greater elite consensus around consolidation. The new debt taken on by the city negated previous objections about absorbing the debt of outlying districts—in fact, it became the outlying districts who were more concerned about absorbing the debt of the central city. At the same time, the railroad was expected to increase land values and economic activity, much of which would benefit the outlying districts who, the new argument for consolidation went, should thus also shoulder some of the costs. There was finally a more general booster element to the consolidation argument, that increasing the size of the city would help Philadelphia compete with other cities, especially New York.[28]

It was at the BoT offices that the Executive Consolidation Committee met to draft the consolidation bill, passed by the legislature in 1854. Under the new city charter, the twenty-nine municipalities (Philadelphia city, nine "incorporated districts," six boroughs, and thirteen townships) were converted into twenty-four electoral districts—"wards"—each of which elected one member to the select council and three members to the common council (city council's upper and lower chambers, respectively). Two particularly densely populated wards (the Seventeenth and Twenty-Third) were given four common council members, resulting in a ninety-eight-member bicameral council. Each ward also elected one member to the board of health, two aldermen (justices of the peace responsible for collecting taxes), two constables, two assessors, and twelve school directors (though four wards maintained prior systems of selecting school directors). Officials elected citywide were the mayor, solicitor, treasurer, controller, receiver of taxes, police marshal, sheriff, coroner, three city commissioners, and sixteen port wardens (eight elected every year to two-year terms).[29] (See Figure 1.3.)

Additional officers elected citywide but who were designated as part of the county separate from the city were the judges, register of wills, recorder of deeds, clerk of quarter sessions, district attorney (DA), and coroner. The 1874 state constitution also made the treasurer, controller, and city commissioners county offices. The purpose of separating city and county offices was to maintain uniformity across all counties for the purposes of state legislation (Philadelphia was and remains the only consolidated city-county in Pennsylvania), and it meant that either type of elected official was subject to different rules (for instance, the legislature set county officers' salaries).[30]

The distinction between city and county offices became a significant hurdle for later reform movements, and vestiges of the county, namely "row offices" such as register of wills, remain a contemporary subject of reform and a dim reflection of the astounding organizational complexity of nineteenth-century city government. Indeed, the 1854 city charter established a government almost completely alien to contemporary observers in the size and bicameralism of the city council and the authority the council exercised through joint standing committees over the departments of finance; water; gasworks; highways, bridges, and sewers; city property and public grounds; police; fire; prisons; schools; and surveys and regulations. The mayor, by contrast, "was little more than a chief of police."[31]

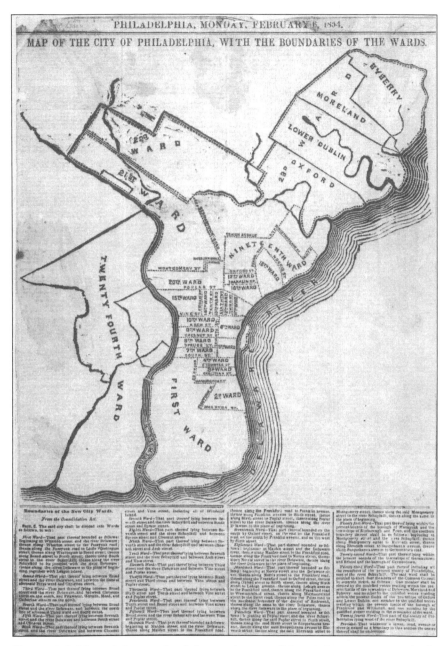

Figure 1.3 Map of the wards of the newly consolidated city-county, overlaid on some of the old municipalities in the county. (From the *Philadelphia Bulletin*, February 6, 1854. In the maps collection of the Free Library of Philadelphia. Courtesy of the Free Library of Philadelphia, Map Collection.)

The mayor elected under the new city charter was Robert Conrad, on the Whig ticket, despite the fact that "the Whig Party was essentially dead, but shrewd people were operating with the skeleton of the defunct."[32] Conrad apparently won with the combined support of Whigs and nativist Know-Nothings, who came together to form the city's Republican Party, though first under the "People's Party" ticket. It was during and after the Civil War that Republicans emerged as the city's dominant party, in large part due to the party's support for a high protective tariff, which was attractive to both the city's working classes and its manufacturers, especially after the 1857 financial panic. It was also, of course, the 1854 consolidation that made this new political coalition possible, as it meant that both elites and working classes were living and voting in the same city.

The Emergence of the Machine-Reform Dichotomy

By the six criteria I provided in the Introduction, the period from the PRR subscription to the city-county consolidation clearly qualifies as a reform cycle: A specific political faction inspired by a new idea of what Philadelphia should be and do gained control of city government in order to implement that idea and radically alter the developmental trajectory of the city. The only sense in which it was not a reform cycle was that the categories of "machine" and "reform" were not yet in wide circulation, though that would soon change. The same predominantly Quaker Whigs who had been supportive of the PRR subscription and consolidation, who then became Republicans, came together to form the Union Club in 1862 (it quickly expanded and was renamed the Union League), largely in reaction to Southern sympathizers in the city's other social and political clubs.[33] Morton McMichael, influential editor and publisher of the *North American* newspaper, a chief organizer and early president of the Union League, and who had earlier served as the chair of the Consolidation Executive Committee, was elected mayor in 1865, signaling "the ascendancy of the Republican party" in the city. Yet, it was a short-lived victory for the city's civic-minded elites. The party quickly became the vehicle for an incipient political machine after the Civil War.[34]

The seeds of the city's political machine were sown in 1835 with the establishment of a city-owned gasworks, governed by a board of trustees elected by the city council. One trustee elected in 1865 was James McManes, an enterprising politician who established a "People's Republican club" in the early 1850s in the densely populated, working class Seventeenth Ward. Given the rapidly growing importance of gas, especially prior to readily available electricity, the trustees found themselves in control of a lucrative asset that McManes converted into a patronage machine by which he controlled council elections, among other things, ensuring that council members continued to reelect him as trustee.[35]

The second pillar of the city's incipient political machine was the Public Buildings Commission (PBC), established in 1870 by the state legislature to oversee the construction of what became the mammoth city hall—planned as the tallest building in the world though beaten by the Eiffel Tower and Washington Monument before its completion in 1901—on the site of what had been Penn (née Centre) Square at the intersection of Broad and Market Streets. Authorized as it was by the state, the city council had no authority over the PBC yet was responsible for paying any PBC contracts, which the commissioners used to establish a vast patronage network that went well beyond city hall, which by itself ultimately cost approximately $25 million, its budget largely acknowledged to have been buttressed by overpayments to contractors who then "kicked back" some of the money to the officials who had given them the contracts.[36]

At the center of the PBC was William Stokely, who had taken a common path into politics by joining a neighborhood fire company. Stokely became a Republican in the 1850s and was elected to the common council in 1860, then to the select council, and became select council president in 1868. His allies in the legislature established the PBC with the mayor and presidents of the select and common councils as ex officio members who were to appoint any other members in the case of vacancies. Ironically, simultaneous to his scheming to control the PBC, Stokely was also campaigning for mayor (successfully—he served from 1871 to 1881) on a reform ticket, promising to establish a professional fire department (in place of the volunteer companies) and to transfer responsibility for the gasworks to a city department.[37]

It was the Gas Trust and, especially, the PBC that inspired "the city's most prominent bankers, lawyers, manufacturers, and merchants" to form the Citizens' Municipal Reform Association (CMRA), in 1871. Historian Peter McCaffery has traced the significant overlap between the membership of the CMRA and the Union League, BoT, and another business association, the Commercial Exchange (founded in 1854 as the Corn Exchange, it changed its name in 1867).[38] There was as well the Reform Club of Philadelphia, organized as an "offshoot" of the CMRA, with a similar membership though established more for social than political purposes.[39] Similarly, banking, mercantile, industrial, and intellectual elites and power brokers such as Anthony Drexel, John Welsh, William Sellers, and J. B. Lippincott formed the Saturday Club that met once a week for dinner and to discuss "what they viewed as the most pressing issues facing the region."[40] The activists behind these various organizations were also the ones who had earlier supported and promoted city-county consolidation and the city's investment in the PRR. As

Peter McCaffery notes, "This tradition, by which government and business formed a partnership for the public good, provided the common ground for businessmen reformers."[41]

New York City's emergent political machine was organized through the Democratic Tammany Hall, and civic-minded elites after the Civil War such as Theodore Roosevelt could thus use the Republican Party as a vehicle for reform. In Philadelphia, the emergent machine was organized under the Republicans, to which the city's business elite were vehemently allegiant, given the party's support for the tariff. The city's reformers thus resorted to supporting "independent" candidates who failed miserably in the 1872 local elections. They had more success in getting reform provisions included into the 1874 state constitution, including restrictions against the kind of special state legislation that had created the PBC, election reforms, and establishing salaries instead of fees for public employees, reducing the potential for bribes.[42]

The organization of various clubs and associations served to carry reform efforts forward with at least some moderate successes, especially when the reformers, virtually all Republicans, allied with the city's Democrats. In the opinion of the eminent British observer of American politics James Bryce, Philadelphia's Democratic Party was equally as corrupt as its GOP but open to an alliance with reformers if it would help them win some elections. And, indeed, reform Democrats won the elections for city controller in 1877 and 1880 (Robert Pattison) and mayor in 1881 (Samuel King, who defeated Stokely, who then ceased to be a major figure in city politics).[43]

Yet, city reform efforts also coincided with and reinforced an effort by Republican state leaders Simon Cameron and his lieutenant Matthew Quay to take control over city patronage resources that had previously been controlled mostly by McManes and Stokely. In 1877, the state legislature, under the direction of Cameron, reestablished the office of Recorder of Philadelphia, a lucrative position that was awarded to Quay.[44] An 1879 state law reduced Philadelphia's debt limit, thereby limiting city expenditures and thus their patronage potential and likely playing a part in King's defeat of Stokely for the mayoralty. Cameron and Quay also helped establish the independent United Republican Association in Philadelphia, intended to undercut the Republican support of Stokely and McManes.[45]

An important vehicle for reform was the 1876 Centennial Exhibition, a remarkable success with more than nine million visitors, it was organized by the same network of civic-minded business elites who had pushed forward the PRR, consolidation, and political reform. As sociologist Jerome Hodos notes, "Centennial promoters and donors were closely allied with or in some cases were the reformers who periodically tried to reshape the city's government. . . . Many had served as founders or officers of organizations like the Union League and the Citizens' Municipal Reform Association."[46] Just as in the case of the PRR subscriptions, it was a leader of the BoT, John Welsh, who, as chair of the Centennial Board of Finance, took chief responsibility for raising money, through shares, for the exposition—a major subscriber to which was the PRR itself, which, by 1876, was one of the largest railroad companies in the world. And Union League biographer Maxwell Whiteman claimed that "the proposal to celebrate the nation's one-hundredth birthday in Philadelphia originated among Union League members."[47]

The centennial was a focusing event that brought together city elites and served to galvanize further reform efforts, such as the Committee of 100, organized in 1880 and credited with getting King elected mayor and getting a new reform charter—known as the "Bullitt Charter" after its primary author, John Bullitt—passed by the state legislature in 1885.[48] The overall purpose of the Bullitt Charter was to centralize and consolidate city functions, thereby fixing what was perceived to be a fragmented and disorganized system, controlled through council committees, that invited corruption and abuse. Thus, the new charter consolidated city functions into nine departments (public safety, public works, receiver of taxes, city treasurer, city controller, law, education, charities, and corrections) and a sinking fund commission, and the mayor (who was restricted to one term) was provided the power to appoint the directors of all the departments, with the exceptions of the elected offices of controller, treasurer, and receiver of taxes.[49]

In short, the 1880s were marked by a reform cycle in the sense that a group of self-identified reformers achieved significant electoral victories against what they characterized as a corrupt ring of politicians, if not a full-fledged "machine," and the reformers made significant changes to city government through a new city charter that reflected the idea of reform by simplifying and consolidating the organizational structure of city government. Yet, by most accounts, the reform effort had run out of steam by the middle of the decade, in part because the reform leaders mostly still had businesses to run, their alliance of convenience with the Democrats had soured, and they were programmatically opposed to creating the kind of political organization that could consistently win elections. In addition, the reform movement was, doubtless, inspired in part by the national "mugwump" Republican reform movement that, after helping get Democrat Grover Cleveland elected president in 1884, lost momentum. Similarly, the Committee of 100 agreed in 1884 to disband and did so in 1886 after passage of the Bullitt Charter, which went into effect in 1887. A successor organization, the Citizens' Municipal Association, was formed in 1886 and reached a peak membership of approximately three hundred but was evidently in decline by the turn of the twentieth century; its greatest success was in serving as something of a watchdog during a large street repaving project.[50]

Moreover, the reform movement of the 1870s and 1880s fails the test of being a reform cycle in the sense that it did not evidently achieve any lasting changes to the city—at least not in the way the reformers had intended. A more cohesive political machine emerged in part because the Bullitt Charter, by centralizing authority, helped Quay (who, by the late 1880s, had succeeded Cameron as state leader and was elected by the legislature to the U.S. Senate in 1887) consolidate the city into the state Republican machine. In Philadelphia, Quay designated as his city-level lieutenant David Martin, a ward leader who also served on the important Republican City Committee.[51]

William Vare, a contemporary of Martin and Quay who was later a leader in the city's political machine, noted that, while Martin "was the most powerful of the group of Republican leaders of the city," there was not yet, in the 1880s, a cohesive machine but instead "various factions within the party, and the bickerings between these elements, along with their weakened alignments against the Democracy of that period, furnished the political strifes of the times."[52] One reflection of the relative fractiousness of the Republicans was Martin's break with Quay when the latter, in 1896, promoted and supported the nomination of state senator Boies Penrose for Philadelphia mayor. In a surprise move, Martin allied himself with other Republicans in the city and throughout the state, in what came to be known as the "Hog Combine," and succeeded in getting city solicitor Charles Warwick nominated to run for mayor over Penrose.[53]

Penrose was a patrician Philadelphian who had started his career working in the law offices of firms whose senior partners were prominent in reform circles, yet he later openly rejected reform, aligned himself with organization Republicans, was elected first to the Pennsylvania House of Representatives, in 1885, and then to the state senate, in 1887, where he became allies with George Vare, who was elected to the state house in 1890. Vare was one of ten children raised on a farm in the hardscrabble "Neck" of South Philadelphia, three of whom—George, William, and Edwin—became partners in various business concerns and city Republican political leaders. Back in Philadelphia, Penrose and Vare allied with Israel Durham, who William Vare described as "then rising in importance in local politics."[54]

Republican dominance in the city and state was finalized in the 1890s. Former Philadelphia controller and Democrat Robert Pattison was serving as governor during the Panic of 1893 and the ensuing recession, and the nomination of populist William Jennings Bryan as the Democrats' 1896 presidential candidate led several prominent Philadelphia Democrats to abandon their party—an instance where a national party realignment did not lead to a local reform cycle but worked to the advantage of the political machine. Quay reestablished his boss status by winning the chairmanship of the state party committee, helped to a great extent by sympathetic delegates nominated from South Philadelphia's First Ward, home of the Vares.

Philadelphia Republicans remained divided into Martin and Durham factions, but Martin's influence was clearly waning. In 1896, George Vare won a state senate seat against a Martin-backed incumbent; in 1897, Durham's nominee was elected sheriff; and, in 1899, Durham ally Samuel Ashbridge was elected mayor. The Vare brothers became the acknowledged leaders of densely packed, working class, and vote-rich South Philadelphia. In 1897, J. Donald Cameron (Simon Cameron's son) retired from the U.S. Senate and in his place the legislature selected Penrose, signaling his ascension to the state party leadership. In 1900, the last Democratic stronghold in the city fell when the Third Congressional District, covering the "river wards" along the Delaware, elected a Republican and remained a party bailiwick into the twentieth century.[55]

Durham centralized party power through the Republican City Committee, largely through rule changes that provided the wards with less power to appoint members to the city committee, nominate candidates for office, and collect patronage. A good share of the patronage that fueled the Republican Organization came through various payments from utilities—gas, electric, and transit—that were also increasingly consolidated in the 1890s. The gasworks had, of course, always been centralized through municipal ownership, but, in 1897, its management was contracted out to a politically connected private firm, United Gas Improvement Company (UGI). In transit, there had, in 1873, been twenty-seven separate companies operating horsecar lines, but the lines were consolidated, first, in 1895, under the United Traction Company and then, in 1902, under the Philadelphia Rapid Transit Company.[56]

Simultaneous to the growth of the Republican Organization was the continuous if muted drumbeat of reform associations led by business leaders and intellectuals—a notably different group than the contractors and utility magnates who benefited from their connections to the machine. For instance, in 1890, a "Committee of Seven" selected at a "town meeting" at the Academy of Music was charged with organizing a "Citizens' Committee of Fifty, to assist in securing for Philadelphia such reforms as are demanded by our citizens, and a more progressive city government." The officers of the Citizens' Committee of Fifty (which actually included seventy-three members) included department store founder Justus Strawbridge, bankers William Rhawn and Francis Reeves, lawyers E. Clinton Rhoades and Joseph De Forrest Junkin, and textile merchant Rudolph Blankenburg. The intellectual bent of the reformers, and the long, even intergenerational, legacy of reform, is suggested by two other officers: Herbert Welsh and Stuart Wood. Welsh had a national reputation as an author and reformer and was one of the founders of the National Civic League and founder of the Indian Rights Association. His father, the prominent merchant John Welsh, had been chair of the 1876 Centennial and a member of the Saturday Club, among other civic ventures. Wood followed into the family mercantile and manufacturing businesses but was also the first person to receive a Ph.D. in economics from Harvard, in 1875.[57] It is notable as well that, of the ten officers of the committee in 1892, four had also been members of the Committee of 100 in the 1880s.[58]

The Citizens' Committee of Fifty endorsed reform goals such as nonpartisan elections, an official ballot, improved public transit, better "school accommodations," and reforms to the city's management of its utilities; worked with reform groups throughout the state to get the legislature to pass an official ballot law; and, in 1892, endorsed 52 of the 157 candidates running for city councils, 25 of whom won.[59] The committee disbanded in 1892, thereby leaving the Citizens' Municipal Association as the remaining general reform group—though there were certainly other reform-oriented organizations, such as settlement houses and the Law and Order Society. Indeed, there was fertile enough ground for reform groups that an alliance of them, the Allied Organizations for Good Government, was established in 1900.[60] Even in the absence of many general reform organizations there were new business groups, most notably the Trades League, established in 1890 (and later to merge with the Chamber of Commerce), which was recognized as a reform group.[61] Trades League founder Howard French, the president of a wholesale drug company and paint manufacturing business, also served as chairman of the Citizens' Committee of Ninety-Five for Good City Government, founded in 1895.[62]

Into the Twentieth Century

Between 1880 and 1900, Philadelphia's population increased by more than 50 percent to nearly 1.3 million people. The city was generally recognized as the country's most important manufacturing center. The 1890s were a period of successive and wrenching economic depressions, labor strife, and political realignment, and, as historian James Wolfinger has noted, "Philadelphia was one of the hotbeds of class conflict . . . witnessing strikes in industries such as elevator construction, the building trades, and textiles."[63] Businesses depended on the city government to keep the peace with workers, through law enforcement and the semiformal welfare state provided mostly through patronage, and to keep systems such as gas and electricity and mass transit running. The city, in turn, had been organized as a party-based "machine" designed to serve the interests of a large coalition that only partially overlapped with the city's business leaders; thus, those business leaders organized and led reform efforts against the perceived (and real) abuses of the machine. As the categories of "machine" and "reform" became institutionalized they would define much of the dynamism in city politics throughout the twentieth century.

2

REFORMING TWENTIETH-CENTURY
PHILADELPHIA

By the twentieth century, "machine" and "reform" were institutionalized categories in Philadelphia politics with clear actors and organizations on either side, though there were overlapping areas of interest and support such as public works that could provide both lucrative contracts and signs of progress. Political stability typically worked to the advantage of the machine (or, as William Vare called it, the "Organization"), as it provided the basis for increasing what economists call "rent-seeking" and what reformers called "corruption," when a group increases its wealth without creating greater wealth for the larger society.

Yet, economic and social changes led to new understandings of what a city was and what its government should do, creating pressure for political change and thus new demands for reform, given voice through the city's press and taken up by a chain of successive and related organizations, the most influential of which were typically controlled by business leaders. At moments when demands for reform resonated with a larger public, reform organizations could expand their coalitions through local networks that mimicked or sometimes simply hijacked the Organization's ward-based networks.

Moments of reform success were evident in the periods roughly demarcated by the years 1905–1916, 1951–1962, and 1991–2000. In the first period, an emergent class of white-collar workers were energized with a new sense of professionalism, blue-collar workers were unionizing and striking, and the larger national reform movement was altering expectations of what city government should be doing. Though the earlier reform cycles of the 1850s and 1880s may have been characterized by class conflict and a distinctly upper-class set of reformers, at least the first two reform cycles of the twentieth century were successful to the extent that they at least momentarily brought together cross-class coalitions. By the 1990s, the ability to create broad cross-class coalitions was limited by the crosscurrents of racial divisions and lower voter turnout.

Divisions in the Republican Organization allowed for moments of reform success, most notably Rudolph Blankenburg's election as mayor in 1911. By the end of Blankenburg's mayoralty, reformers had themselves devolved into factions and the Organization reestablished its control. Thus, an ostensible reform success in 1919—passage of a new city charter—ended up helping the Penrose faction of the Organization. In the late 1940s, a new set of reform activists, energized by a vision of the city as a center of industry and technology infused with federal dollars and supportive of civil rights, allied with the Democratic Party and overthrew the remnants of the Republican machine that had been ravaged by the Great Depression, New Deal, and World War II. The postwar reform cycle was defined by the most dramatic party realignment since the Civil War; in just a few years, Democrats became the city's dominant party, under which a new machine took shape by the end of Richardson Dilworth's mayoralty.

Philadelphia after World War II was defined by an increasing Black population, a declining white population, increasingly powerful municipal unions, and economic decline. Black politicians divided roughly into traditional reform and machine categories, with the machine version prominent in District Council 33 (DC 33) of the American Federation of State, County, and Municipal Employees (AFSCME). DC 33 provided much of the foil for a new reform cycle inaugurated by the election of Ed Rendell, as mayor in 1991, who confronted a fiscal crisis rivaling that of the 1930s with policies inspired by the trend of reinventing government. Yet, neither Rendell nor other observers characterized him as a reform mayor. In conclusion, I argue that viewing Rendell as a reform mayor provides a window on the extent to which the potential for and nature of political reform had changed over the twentieth century.

The Republican Organization and Progressive Reform

The Republican Organization, led statewide by Matthew Quay and in Philadelphia by Israel Durham, dominated city politics at the turn of the twentieth century. Durham centralized authority through the Republican City Committee, composed of the city's forty-eight ward leaders, where patronage was used to maintain allegiance. Patronage resources were generated by a city whose population increased by 20 percent between 1900 and 1910, to 1,549,008 people, where increasing tax revenues paid for roads, buildings, water and sewer lines, streetlights, a subway, trash collection, street cleaning, police, and teachers, all of which generated jobs and contracts. Despite the ostensible consolidation of city functions under the 1885 charter, there were thirty-one city government departments "and scores of bureaus and divisions" that included approximately twenty-three thousand jobs (which an ineffectual civil service system hardly protected) and numerous contracts. Utility companies that relied on city contracts and franchises, such as Philadelphia Rapid Transit (PRT), Philadelphia Electric, and United Gas Improvement, provided additional patronage resources.[1]

Electoral fraud, voter intimidation, and voter apathy also helped maintain Organization control, as described in muckraking journalist Lincoln Steffens's 1903 *McClure's* article in which he famously called Philadelphia "corrupt and contented."[2] The city's electorate was by all accounts genuinely allegiant to the Republican Party, especially its support for the protective tariff. Thus, reformers who sought to win elections ran not as Democrats but in Republican "independent" parties, such as "the City Party (1905–7), the Keystone party (1910–15), the Washington party (1912–16), and the Franklin party (1915–1916)."[3]

Yet, the Organization was never a monolith and the wards could never be fully centralized. Ward leaders delivered votes for Organization candidates and were rewarded with patronage that they used to maintain control in their wards. For instance, more than a thousand Republican committeemen—the politicians immediately underneath ward leaders who were responsible for the "divisions" into which the wards were divided—were employed by the city. Patronage recipients were, thus, primarily loyal to their ward leaders. Ward leaders took a percentage of city salaries as a kickback to ward coffers (as did the city committee), and they were also able to keep tabs on patronage recipients by requiring that they live in the wards. Ambitious ward leaders, who themselves often held elective offices, looked to increase their power, and "bitter factional disputes were common, leaving contests for smaller offices and committee positions hotly challenged."[4]

Even at the top of the Organization there were factions, unpredictable elections and nominating conventions, and defectors. One consequential fault line lay between the Vare brothers (George, William, and Edwin) who had become wealthy contractors and the dominant political force in the densely packed central and southern portions of the city, and Boies Penrose, who became the state boss after Quay died, in 1904, and who, as William Vare put it in his 1933 memoir, "was to definitely assert himself . . . and to invite

Figure 2.1 Bain News Service, Publisher. *Boies Penrose*, ca. 1915. [Between and ca. 1920] (Photograph. Library of Congress, Prints and Photographs Division, [reproduction number, e.g., LC-B2-1234], Washington, DC.)

a long series of conflicts with the independent voters of the city and State in consequence."[5] (See Figure 2.1.)

Overriding the Vares' preference for a candidate, Durham nominated his protégé, district attorney (DA) John Weaver, for mayor in 1903. According to Vare, Weaver made a "deep impression of his sincerity upon the independents" and was easily elected.[6] One popular magazine described Weaver as "honest and clean-lived, a Sunday-school teacher and a religious man. Politically, he was only a brass door-plate."[7] Yet, Steffens noted that "he was the nominee of the ring; and the ring men have confidence in him. But so have the people, and Mr. Weaver makes fair promises."[8] (See Figure 2.2.)

Steffens's article may have put some pressure on the mayor to break with the Organization. Whatever the case, the break occurred in 1905 over a new lease of the city's gasworks to UGI, under which the company was to pay the city $25 million over three years for the right to operate and collect revenues from the gasworks for seventy-five years—a deep discount from what UGI had been previously paying, which over seventy years would have amounted to well over $100 million.[9] As historian Lloyd Abernathy put it, "The bulk payments would provide a handsome kitty with which to award municipal contracts to firms associated with Durham and his friends."[10]

Weaver signaled that he would veto the lease, and Durham intended to gather enough council votes to override the veto. As William Vare explained it, "These rough-shod tactics gave the independents their excuse for shout-

Figure 2.2 Campaign badge to be worn to the polls on February 17, 1903, distributed as a supplement to the *Philadelphia Inquirer*, with images of Theodore Roosevelt on horseback and winning Republican mayoral candidate John Weaver. (Library of Congress, Prints and Photographs Division, Washington, DC.)

ing 'steal.'"[11] Vare's vivid description of the extent of public outrage belied Steffens's depiction of a contented public:

> Citizens' associations throughout Philadelphia began to assemble, with growing attendance, and to forward to Councils resolutions of protest against the railroading of the gas lease ordinance. . . . Crowds lined the South Broad Street approaches to City Hall and cheered Mayor Weaver on his way to and from lunch. The entrances to the galleries of Councils were practically mobbed by thousands of citizens and the sessions became even more disorderly. . . . Delegations in large numbers, in some instances regular mobs, waited upon Councilmanic members in front of their residences and demanded explanations.[12]

The muckraking *Munsey's Magazine* noted that "women, who have unusual influence in this city of homes, took part by declaring a boycott upon the councilmen's wives. . . . Councilmen who owned stores or saloons found their trade dwindling below the profit line."[13]

More so than the gas lease veto, however, Weaver (in William Vare's words) "crossed the Rubicon of Philadelphia politics" when he fired the directors of Public Safety and Public Works and replaced them with professionals not allegiant to the Organization—a major blow to patronage resources.[14] The Department of Public Safety, for instance, included the bureaus of police, fire, building inspection, traffic engineering, corrections, health, and city property, the fire marshal, the electrical bureau, and the city's medical division and highway traffic board; the Department of Public Works was responsible for nearly every aspect of building and maintaining the city water and sewer systems, streets, highways, parks, and public buildings.[15] Vare claimed that "hundreds" of city employees "saved their jobs by swearing in for the new reform regime."[16]

The gas lease revolt reflected widespread resentment among a broad swath of groups. Beyond the contractors and utility companies who depended on the Organization, the numerous and diverse businesses in the city most likely saw the machine as simply inefficient. As one group of prominent businessmen put it in 1904, the machine "enormously increases the cost of carrying on the business of the city, and it decreases the returns to the citizens from such cost."[17] And while the Organization made a show of providing welfare-oriented services to city residents, it was certainly not lost on many of them that those services were allocated unfairly, that city patronage jobs were often badly paid and required kickbacks, and that staying employed depended on the whims of ward leaders.[18]

There are also reasons to think that reformers had gained deeper competitive advantages against the machine. First, Philadelphians were caught up in the national reform movement, galvanized by Theodore Roosevelt's 1904 presidential campaign and election—especially since Roosevelt was a Republican—and his themes of the dangers of large corporations and the benefits of unions and government regulations. At the state level, Governor Pennypacker, under pressure from reform groups, also supported reform legislation such as party primaries, "personal registration of voters, a stricter civil service code to prohibit political activity by city employees, and a corrupt practices act."[19]

Second, the press had become a more effective reform tool. Steffens's 1903 exposé was, for instance, published in one of the country's most widely circulated magazines. In Philadelphia, at least three of the five major newspapers were reform-oriented, most notably the *North American* under the editorship of Edwin Van Valkenburg, the former political manager for department store magnate and reformer John Wanamaker. In 1899, Van Valkenburg convinced Wanamaker's son to purchase the *North American* and make him editor. As Steffens described Van Valkenburg, "He knew everybody and everything. He printed everything, too. Threatened with assassination, he simply moved his desk out of range of his window and went right on getting and publishing the evidence, the libelous, uncontradicted facts."[20]

Third, as the broad response to the gas lease indicates, reformers had expanded beyond elite clubs and committees. The Municipal League, for instance, was established in 1891, mimicked the political parties' ward system, and "represented a new kind of elite activism, one in which the participants, more interested in political issues than social activities, strove to overcome the shortcomings of their predecessors by founding clubs and leagues of a permanent rather than ad hoc nature."[21] In its final act before disbanding, in 1904, the Municipal League hosted a public meeting at the Bourse (a commodities exchange established in 1891) out of which came a "Committee of Seven" (different from the earlier committee discussed in Chapter 1), including five business leaders (soap maker Samuel Fels, attorney Frank Prichard, physician and property developer George Woodward, manufacturer W. H. Pfahler, and merchant Frederick Strawbridge), and one union president (Alfred Calvert, of the typographers).[22]

The Committee of Seven organized a new broad-based but still elite-driven group, the Committee of Seventy, which, in turn, served as the organizational springboard for the more broad-based City Party, with which Mayor Weaver affiliated himself.[23] As William Vare noted, the City Party was formed with the help of "the more practical politicians who joined the crusade against the Organization." In 1905, City Party candidates were elected to several county offices (sheriff, coroner, and two county commissioners), which Vare described as "the worst defeat sustained by the Organization in its entire history."[24]

Fourth, reformist ideology and orientation was fostered through the growth of white-collar professionalism and clerical employment. Clerks worked for the kinds of proprietors who were often businessmen-reformers, such as Wanamaker and the Strawbridges, and they were often educated in the same "scientific management" principles, made famous by Philadelphian Frederick Taylor, that inspired reformers' efficiency goals.[25] Rising educational standards for white-collar workers were reflected in new educational institutions designed to be accessible and focused on upward mobility, such as the Union Business College (founded 1865), the University of Pennsylvania's Wharton School (1881), Temple College (1887), and the Drexel Institute of Art, Science, and Industry (1891). Wharton was a center for progressive reform through the 1910s,[26] and Drexel's second president was an associate and disciple of Taylor and modeled the school's curriculum on scientific management principles.[27]

Weaver left the City Party when it refused to back him for governor, and City Party candidates did not fare well in 1906 or 1907. George Vare died in 1908 and his brother Edwin was elected to his state senate seat. By 1907, Penrose, state senator James McNichol, and the Vares, formed an uneasy alliance, sharing Organization leadership.[28] Meanwhile, reformers, in 1909, established a new think tank–type organization, the Philadelphia Bureau of Municipal Research (PBMR), largely through the efforts of George Woodward, a nonpracticing physician, a real estate developer who shaped much of the city's bucolic and upper-income Chestnut Hill neighborhood (where Frederick Taylor lived), a state senator from 1919 to 1947, and a member of the Committee of Seven (another member, Samuel Fels, provided much of the early funding for the PBMR) and Committee of Seventy. The PBMR was modeled after the New York Bureau of Municipal Research; twelve additional bureaus were established in other cities by 1914. The PBMR was distinct for the prominence of business groups on its board of directors, on which two seats a piece were reserved for the Chamber of Commerce, BoT, and the Merchants and Manufacturers Association.[29]

It was Philadelphia's business leaders along with white-collar professionals such as physicians and lawyers who typically led the reform groups. Large companies, especially those such as the utilities that depended on city franchises, were less active. Where most businesses, reformers, and the Organization could find consensus was on large public works projects, many of which were also designed to accommodate increasing automobile traffic, such as a parkway proposed in 1904 to run northwest from city hall to a proposed new art museum, cutting through a broad swath of working-class homes and factories; a new central library building along the parkway; large parks running along Cobbs Creek at the western edge of the city and the Tacony and Pennypack Creeks in the northeast, and a new boulevard that would run through the northeast, named after Theodore Roosevelt.[30]

A large manufacturing city was also defined by labor activism. In the same year as the PBMR was formed, PRT workers went on strike. The PRT was unpopular, and the strike had broad support but was disruptive and violent, especially against out-of-town streetcar operators brought in to break the strike.[31] For Penrose, McNichol, and the Vares (all PRT allies and sympathizers), the strike threatened to benefit reform candidates in the 1909 Republican primary, most notably for DA, where D. Clarence Gibboney (leader of the reformist Law and Order Society who Vare called a "pet of the Van Valkenburg element") was running against Penrose protégé Samuel Rotan. McNichol worked with the PRT to offer concessions, ending the strike. In what should have been an easy election for the Organization, Rotan won only a narrow victory against Gibboney, in both the Republican primary and general election (Gibboney also ran in and won the Democratic primary—a practice banned by state law in 1935).[32] After the election, PRT management sought to crush the transit workers' union, leading to a new strike in 1910, which expanded into a general strike of approximately 140,000 workers across multiple industries, organized by the Central Labor Union.[33]

The year following the general strike, Keystone Party candidate and long-standing reform figure Rudolph Blankenburg was narrowly elected mayor against Organization candidate George Earle Jr. Blankenburg's victory is often attributed to the fact that Earle, a Penrose ally, ran against William Vare in the Republican mayoral primary; thus, the Vares failed to turn out voters for Earle in the general election. In his memoir, Vare half-heartedly denied this explanation, claimed exceptional enthusiasm for the Keystone ticket beyond Blankenburg, and "numerous wounds still unhealed from the two trolley strikes."[34] In short, Blankenburg's election reflects both the activism of business-oriented reformers and the reformers' ability to extend their reach beyond elite circles, and at least a temporary alliance between reformers and labor. Another notable aspect, alluded to in the preceding quote from *Munsey's*, was the role of women in Philadelphia reform efforts, in particular, the "dense network of women's clubs and organizations" led by Blankenburg's wife Lucretia, which "served as her husband's de facto political organization during the campaign's home stretch."[35]

Blankenburg was active in practically every major reform effort dating back to the Committee of 100 (see Chapter 1). There has been some brief academic debate regarding the composition of these reform groups,[36] but, in general, the Progressive Era reformers were a mix of older mugwumps, upper-middle-class professionals, and some scions from old Philadelphia families, who had established organizations that followed in a long and largely continuous path that can be traced as far back as the BoT's prominent role in financing the PRR in the 1840s and the 1854 city-county consolidation, through the founding of the Union League in 1862, CMRA in 1871, Committee of 100 in 1880, Municipal League in 1891, Committee of Seventy in 1904, and the PBMR in 1909. As historian Bonnie Fox noted, "The younger members of the Committee of 100 were to become the leaders of the groups that followed."[37] The organizational infrastructure of successive reform groups provided an intergenerational avenue by which civic-oriented elites who were invested in the idea of progress could find their compatriots, from which broader alliances could sometimes be forged and thus larger political and social movements could sometimes spring when the timing was right.

The Organization Cracks

Weaver's defection from the Organization and Blankenburg's election can be seen collectively as two parts of a reform cycle that reflected the ideals of white-collar professionalism, dissatisfaction with flagrant corruption, and a burgeoning labor movement. Yet, the extent to which reformers managed to make any lasting changes to city government in this period is generally considered to have been negligible. As his wife Lucretia conceded, "It is often said that 'Mr. Blankenburg was a good Mayor, but he did not accomplish much by way of city improvements.'"[38] Yet, even as the city council blocked many of his plans, Blankenburg managed to establish a milk inspection program and office of baby health, limited party assessments on city employee salaries, improved budgeting and contracting, and advanced various public works, though the parkway and art museum projects stalled. He also created resentment in reform ranks by refusing to use patronage to help build the statewide Washington Party to support Roosevelt's 1912 presidential bid, and he failed to lower the price of gas (a campaign promise), putting him at odds with Van Valkenberg and fracturing the progressive coalition.[39]

Organization candidates swept the 1913 county elections, and, in 1914, Boies Penrose beat Washington Party candidate Gifford Pinchot in Pennsylvania's first election for U.S. Senate. Hoping to distance themselves from the Washington Party's defeats, Philadelphia's reformers reorganized under the Franklin Party, though several factions failed to support its 1915 mayoral candidate, who captured only one-third of the vote. The following year, eighty prominent city reformers "issued a statement disbanding the Franklin party and declaring their intention to return to the Republican fold."[40]

Blankenburg died in 1918 and public attention had shifted to World War I and then the Spanish flu. Yet, just as reform seemed largely dormant, reform groups allied with Penrose against the Vare faction of the Organization and scored possibly their most important victory, a new city charter passed by the state legislature in 1919. The new charter changed the city council from a bicameral body of 145 members elected by wards to a unicameral body of 21 members (the number actually varied slightly since they were elected by state senate districts, with each district getting one member per twenty thousand people). Reducing the council size was a standard reform measure, recommended, for instance, in the National Civic League's model city charter, but subsuming the wards into larger electoral districts was also designed to weaken the Vares' ward-based power, though the wards remained electoral districts for party elections. Another reform provision, requiring the city "to do its own street-cleaning and repairing and waste removal" rather than contract for those services, was also aimed at reducing a major source of the Vares' revenue. Other standard reform measures, such as at-large, nonpartisan, or proportional representation elections, were left out of the charter, and county officials also remained exempt from civil service rules.[41]

One legacy of the 1919 charter was the Charter Reform Committee (later named the City Charter Committee). Established by the Committee of Seventy, it persisted well beyond 1919 to become, as described by one of its members, "one of those nonpartisan organizations of private and independent citizens from all sections of the community which, like the Citizens' Union in New York and the Charter Committee in Cincinnati, have contributed so much to the promotion of better municipal government in the larger cities."[42]

Penrose's candidate J. Hampton Moore beat the Vares' candidate in the first Republican mayoral primary under the new charter, and Moore was elected mayor in the general election by over 80 percent. In the council, eleven of the twenty-one newly elected members were Penrose allies.[43] Yet, Penrose died in 1921 (his successor in the U.S. Senate, George Wharton Pepper, stayed out of city politics) and, in 1923, Vare allies won the majority of council seats and the mayoralty, which went to Freeland Kendrick. In 1926, the last living and most influential Vare, William, sought the traditional post of state party bosses and ran for the U.S. Senate, which he won exclusively by the overwhelming votes he received in Philadelphia.[44] He was, however, charged with electoral fraud and the Senate refused to seat him—a humiliation that Vare suggested led to a stroke in 1928, followed by his weaker health (he died in 1934), during which the Organization broke into factions of ward leaders fighting over who would be the new city leader.[45] (See Figure 2.3.)

Three notable features of the 1920s were economic prosperity (despite the fact that Philadelphia's textiles industry was in decline as manufacturers moved

Figure 2.3 Freeland Kendrick (*left*) and William Vare (*right*) in 1927. Kendrick was mayor from 1924 to 1928. Behind Kendrick and Vare appear to be members of the Republican City Committee. *Mayor Kendrick and Sen. Vare*, January, 15, 1927. (Photograph. Library of Congress, Prints and Photographs Division, [reproduction number, e.g., LC-F82-1234], Washington, DC.)

south in search of cheaper labor and cotton), the prohibition of alcohol under the Eighteenth Amendment (leading to new issues of law enforcement, organized crime, and corruption), and the rise of automobile use (officials counted one hundred thousand cars in the city in 1918).[46] With ample tax revenues, major public works proceeded rapidly under mayors Moore and Kendrick, including the city's second subway line, the Delaware River Bridge (later named after Benjamin Franklin), a new art museum, new public library central branch building, and scores of new school buildings and parks. The city hosted a massive sesquicentennial celebration in 1926, which, though generally considered a failure and financial fiasco, catalyzed development in what were previously the marshlands and hardscrabble farms of South Philadelphia, thereby opening up new housing to meet the needs of a city whose population increased by 7 percent in the 1920s (to 1.95 million in 1930) and was sprawling out to previously undeveloped land, most notably in the northeast, which was made more accessible to cars through Roosevelt Boulevard.

These ambitious public works projects were completed just in time for the 1929 stock market crash. The electoral realignment that swept Demo-

crats into office nationally after the onset of the Great Depression was muted in Pennsylvania, one of only six states to cast a majority vote for Herbert
Hoover in 1932. Yet, electoral and political dynamics in the city and state
changed fundamentally as "400,000 Philadelphians switched their affiliation
to the Democratic Party between 1932 and 1935." Facing a budget shortfall
and a swift public backlash after they attempted to raise taxes, the mayor and
city council were forced to lay off thirty-five hundred city workers in 1931—
a clear blow to patronage resources. Democrats won majorities in the Pennsylvania House of Representatives and State Senate in 1934 and 1936, respectively. Roosevelt won sweeping majorities in the city and state in 1936,
winning majorities in forty-two of what were by then the city's fifty wards,
and Democrats won in all of the city's congressional districts.[47]

The city's Democrats were rejuvenated under the leadership of brick
magnate John Kelly, real estate mogul Albert Greenfield, and *Public Record*
publisher J. David Stern, and flush with New Deal patronage, most of which
flowed through the state party into federal facilities such as the Navy Yard,
Mint, and Post Office.[48] Kelly ran for mayor in 1935 and lost to Republican
candidate and former city controller Samuel Davis Wilson, yet, the margin
of victory, 53 to 47 percent, was the slimmest for a Republican since the 1880s.
And Wilson was only nominally a Republican; he had supported Roosevelt
in 1932, was elected controller on the independent Town Meeting party ticket, and had made an agreement of convenience with the city GOP that if he
was elected mayor as a Republican he would cede most of the accompanying
patronage to the party.[49] As mayor, Wilson allied himself with Kelly (at that
point, Democratic City Committee chair and state secretary of revenue) and
encouraged city workers to switch to the Democratic Party.[50] (See Figure 2.4.)

A new threat to patronage was municipal unionization. Teamsters attempted to organize sanitation workers and ultimately organized a strike in
1937. Mayor Wilson offered pay raises but supported unionization through
a competitor to the Teamsters, the Municipal Workers Union. Layoffs and
wage cuts led Teamsters and Municipal Workers Union members to jointly
strike in 1938, resulting in eight days of "Garbage Riots" that compelled the
city to meet all the strikers' demands, including official recognition of the
Municipal Workers Union, which affiliated with the newly formed AFSCME
as Local 222.[51]

While sanitation workers were organizing and striking, the combination
of the city's heavy debt (generated by ambitious, patronage-laden public works)
and declining tax revenues resulted in a $20 million municipal deficit in
1937. Mayor Wilson proposed a nine-month budget, with the hope that the
final three months might be filled in by state assistance and unspecified cost
savings. Governor George Earle resisted the idea of state aid and city controller

Figure 2.4 City controller and Republican mayoral candidate S. Davis Wilson (*center*), in 1935, with city councilman Clarence K. Crossan (*left*) and Edwin R. Cox, chairman of the Republican City Committee (*right*). (Special Collections Research Center, Temple University Libraries, Philadelphia, PA.)

Robert White refused to certify the partial budget. The mayor and city council made some genuine budget cuts but also inflated their revenue projections, leading to new budget crises at the ends of 1937 and 1938, by which time the state legislature had authorized, and city council passed, a new income tax, paid by both city and suburban residents who worked in the city, intended to be temporary but which is today the city's single largest source of revenue.[52]

The fiscal crisis had many of the signs at least of the conditions for a reform cycle. First, it aroused public indignation. City council alternately targeted property, sales, and wages for a new tax, mobilizing a wide array of groups: Unions opposed a wage tax, businesses opposed a sales tax, and real estate interests opposed a property tax. The indignation was reminiscent of that which attended the 1905 gas lease, with "the Council galleries . . . filled to the last seat . . . while hundreds of angry citizens pressed at the iron gates in the fourth and fifth-floor corridors of City Hall. . . . Dozens of pickets marched around the building with placards denouncing the income tax, the sales tax and demanding that 'bums' be thrown out of City Hall."[53]

Second, much of the budget debate centered on eliminating patronage, especially in the county offices that were exempt from the city's civil service. City controller Robert White, a Democrat with mayoral ambitions, publicized patronage positions when he rejected the proposed 1937 budget. The focus on eliminating patronage came, in part, from the Committee of Seventy and PBMR, but the most active reform group was the newer Pennsylvania Economy League (PEL), founded as a statewide organization in 1935, closely aligned with the PBMR (with which it shared a corporate charter) and focused on consulting with the state and local governments over efficiencies in response to declining revenues.[54] The league was organized into local committees (later called divisions), and the head of PEL's Philadelphia committee was Howard Cooper Johnson, vice president and general counsel at Strawbridge and Clothier, president of the Philadelphia Merchants Association, and a member of the Union League.[55]

At the height of the budget crisis in 1936, Mayor Wilson, attempting to pass the buck, commented that "he had already effected many economies recommended by the Pennsylvania Economy League, but that he could not eliminate any additional jobs until the League completed further studies."[56] In response, and reflecting the class structure of reform, the heads of eight county offices—the target of many proposed layoffs—"bitterly assailed the Economy League as controlled by big business interests and hinted that municipal taxes on big business would be preferable to the firing of low-paid county workers."[57] Possibly because he was looking for a new group of respectable experts whose recommendations would focus more on new taxes than PEL's recommended layoffs, Wilson organized a Municipal Advisory Finance Commission in 1937, known as the "Gates Commission" after its chair, Penn president Thomas Gates. The two other commissioners, who oversaw a "corps of research workers," were John McCarthy, vice president of the Real Estate Trust Company, and Richard A. Lansburgh, an officer of PEL's Philadelphia committee, former state secretary of labor and industry, a Penn economics instructor, and a disciple of Taylor and scientific management.[58]

Third, the fiscal crisis revived charter reform efforts—which, with the persistence of the City Charter Committee and legislators such as Woodward, had never actually died. Reformers had proposed significant charter amendments in 1929 and 1931, with no success, but the budget impasse of 1936 combined with a Democratic governor and Democratic majorities in both legislative chambers opened a new window of opportunity. At the start of the 1937 session, John Kelly proposed a state constitutional amendment consolidating city and county offices—which would have eliminated a key source of city GOP patronage—and a new Philadelphia charter commission. Democratic state senator Harry Shapiro, from Philadelphia, opened up a sweeping inquiry into city finances, considered "in some circles" to be "a forerunner to the establishment of a new city charter."[59] The legislature approved a new charter commission, composed of "public officials, representatives of employers and labor, and prominent citizens," who proposed standard reforms such as a council-manager system, a smaller council elected at-large through proportional representation, and a stronger civil service.[60]

Yet, Republicans captured majorities in both legislative chambers in 1938 and city-county consolidation and the city charter died in committee in 1939. Mayor Wilson also died that year, and, after a brief mayoralty by council president George Connell, the reliably Republican Robert Lamberton was elected over former controller Robert White by nearly the same margin (53 to

47 percent) as Wilson had beat Kelly in 1935. In 1941, Lamberton died; council president Bernard Samuel became mayor and went on to win the mayoralty twice against upper-class Democratic reform candidates: Former foreign service officer William Bullitt in 1943 (54–46 percent), and attorney and war veteran Richardson Dilworth in 1947 (56–44 percent).[61] Thus Republicans maintained their electoral majorities, but they were slim compared to the majorities of over 80 percent that GOP mayoral candidates enjoyed prior to the Great Depression. (See Figure 2.5.)

Despite these defeats, reform ranks were rejuvenated. One member of the City Charter Committee noted that their efforts had brought together "more than a hundred organized civic, business, trade, and professional groups" and had led to the creation of women's reform groups "in most of the wards of the city. A separate organization, the Charter League, undertook particularly to interest the younger people in the charter."[62] Kirk Petshek, who served as city economist after World War II, noted of the 1939 effort that "the names of many of the young people who worked on that City Charter Committee appear repeatedly in the annals of the later Philadelphia reform."[63]

One active reformer and stalwart Democrat involved in both the City Charter Committee and the PBMR was Walter Phillips. Part of an old patrician family, Phillips graduated from Harvard Law School, returned to Philadelphia in 1936, and was one of the chief founders or members of nearly every influential reform organization in the 1940s and 1950s. The City Charter Committee disbanded in 1939, and, in its place, Phillips took the lead in founding the City Policy Committee (CPC), which brought together "young, political outsiders," though it also had a distinct elite and professional character; its members consisted of the same types—"bankers, businessmen, architects, lawyers, planners"—as previous organizations.[64] As Petshek noted, its "restricted membership," of approximately eighty members, "made an invitation to join it a coveted honor."[65] There was also substantial overlap in the membership between the CPC and other reform groups, most notably the PBMR, where Phillips was a board member.

Besides Phillips, three CPC members of note were attorneys Richardson Dilworth and Joseph Clark, who would later both be elected mayors, and Edmund Bacon, who had just returned home to Philadelphia after working as a city planner in Flint, Michigan, to work as managing director of the Philadelphia Housing Association, another Progressive Era reform group, founded in 1916. Possibly due to Bacon's influence, the CPC focused on establishing a professional city planning commission and to do so partnered with the Lawyers' Council on Civic Affairs and the Junior Board of Commerce to form the Joint Committee on City Planning.[66]

Figure 2.5 A meeting of the Republican City Committee in 1936. Standing is councilman George Connell who, in 1939, served as acting mayor after the death of Mayor S. Davis Wilson. (Special Collections Research Center, Temple University Libraries, Philadelphia, PA.)

In response to Mayor Samuel's opposition to a new planning commission, the Joint Committee on City Planning became an "Action Committee," enlisted the support of power brokers, most notably Drexel and Company partner Edward Hopkinson, initiated a grassroots campaign, and secured "the support of fifty-five organizations," including "good government organizations, labor unions, civic associations, women's groups, religious organizations, and others that had no clear connection to the issue but felt it would be beneficial to the public good." This effort compelled the mayor and council to approve a new and more substantial commission, established in 1943 with Hopkinson as chairman. In the same year, Phillips and Bacon institutionalized the relationship between the new commission and the "numerous grassroots organizations . . . supportive of bringing planning to Philadelphia" by establishing a successor organization to the Action Committee, the Citizens' Council on City Planning (CCCP).[67]

By the end of 1943, Bacon, Clark, and Dilworth were serving in the military. The final years of World War II were an interregnum in the emergent reform movement, which after the war would be rejuvenated by new energy, new organizations, and new federal programs, but which also relied on the long tradition of interconnected groups that stretched back into the nineteenth century. Just as the Committee of 100 and the Municipal League had served as the organizational and civic infrastructure from which the Committee of Seventy, PBMR, and the City Charter Committee were launched, these newer organizations served the same role in facilitating the emergence of the CPC and CCCP. These various and successive groups had had moments of opportunity for building broader coalitions and achieving some electoral successes in the 1900s and 1910s, and then suffered a series of failed charter reform efforts in the 1920s and 1930s. The period of approximately two decades after the war served as another window of opportunity for a full-fledged moment of political reform.

Political Reform after World War II

Philadelphia's political parties regrouped and reorganized after the war. Leadership in the GOP was shared through an uneasy and uninspired alliance between Austin Meehan, elected sheriff in 1944 and leader of the Thirty-Fifth Ward that covered the lightly developed but rapidly growing northeastern section of the city; William Meade, chair of the board of revision of taxes and elected Republican City Committee chair in 1945; and Morton Witkin, chair of the county board of elections. Among the Democrats, Michael Bradley, city committee chairman, allied himself with his party's reform branch and helped get Dilworth nominated as the party's 1947 mayoral candidate.[68] Dilworth lost but overperformed in several keys wards and ran an innovative and aggressive campaign that captured public attention with forceful charges of corruption, helping to increase turnout by 17 percent over the previous mayoral election.[69] In that same year, voting machines replaced paper ballots, reducing the potential for electoral fraud,[70] and, in 1949, Dilworth was elected city treasurer while his political partner Clark was elected controller. Democrats also won "two vacant councilmanic seats, four magistrates' posts, and the four row offices."[71]

Democratic victories in 1949 resulted, in part, from revelations of corruption by a "Committee of Fifteen" organized by Mayor Samuel in 1948 to justify new taxes to pay for a wage increase to municipal workers, whose bargaining power had grown as AFSCME expanded to cover more than seven thousand city employees, organized into locals (that is, separate union branches typically divided by city department) across an increasing number of departments under the umbrella of DC 33. Samuel appointed business leaders to his committee and expected it would repeat the Gates Commission's recommendation from the 1930s of new taxes, which it did not. With the help of private businesses, PBMR, and PEL, the Committee of Fifteen issued a series of damning reports, highlighting gross inefficiencies and criminal corruption, leading to dismissals, arrests, indictments, suicides, further investigations—and a wave of negative publicity that provided a new window of opportunity for reformers.[72]

The nearly reflexive first reform step was once again pursuing charter changes in the legislature, promoted by largely the same groups that had done so in the 1930s—PEL, PBMR, the Committee of Seventy, the Chamber of Commerce—though joined by the CPC, CCCP, and two newer groups: The Greater Philadelphia Movement (GPM), established in 1949 and consisting of some 150 elites, including union and civic leaders, but dominated by the "big-business, financial and legal interests which started it,"[73] and the Philadelphia chapter of Americans for Democratic Action (ADA) formed in 1947 by liberal intellectuals and labor leaders who had split with Communists in a predecessor organization. The ADA was a distinct and crucial component of postwar reform successes in its role of bringing together labor, the Democratic Party, and the more upper-class, business-oriented reformers who composed the cores of practically every other reform group. As one former member recalled, "Many ADA members, as part of their perceived political mission, made it a point to occasionally drop in at their local Democratic ward club in order to maintain relationships with the ward leaders and the committeemen."[74]

The GPM's most active members were part of the "inner circle" of the city's "power structure" and represented companies such as the PRR, Pennsylvania Company for Banking and Trusts, and major law firms.[75] The group was established to promote reform efforts, including charter reform, but also out of a general concern for the regional economy, which was showing the first signs of deindustrialization, starting with large layoffs at government installations such as the Navy Yard and Frankford Arsenal, and at companies with military contracts such as Cramp's Shipyard and Midvale Steel. Manufacturers (notably a minor part of GPM membership), especially, started moving out of the city, both to the neighboring suburbs where land was cheaper and to Southern and southwestern states where unions were less powerful and labor less expensive. The percentage of manufacturing jobs in the Philadelphia region located in the central city declined from more than 60 percent to just 50 percent as early as 1943. And while 4 percent of the country's industrial workforce had been employed in Philadelphia prior to World War II, that percentage had been cut in half by the end of the war.[76]

In response to the city's political scandals, in 1949, the legislature approved state constitutional amendments allowing for city-county consolidations (subject to a referendum), and authorizing a charter commission for Philadelphia (established on a two-thirds vote of the city council or a petition of twenty thousand voters), consisting of nine members selected by the council president and six by the mayor, that would have responsibility for drafting a "home rule" charter to be submitted to voters in a special election in April 1951. The influence of the GPM was evident in the fact that the majority of charter commission members were selected from a list developed by the GPM, and six GPM members were appointed to the commission.[77] The GPM also took the lead role in creating the Citizens' Charter Committee, which brought together "522 member organizations" and "set up ward and district committees, a speaker's bureau, a publicity bureau and other campaign activities."[78]

From its establishment in 1949 until it released the final draft charter in February 1951, the charter commission held at least seven public hearings, and the Citizens' Charter Committee led a massive publicity drive, including sample ballots and various explanatory materials distributed directly to households, public schools to be used as teaching lessons, and the daily press, which had changed dramatically since the 1930s: In 1925, the *North American* had been absorbed by the *Public Ledger*, which was, in turn, absorbed in 1934 by the *Inquirer*. In 1936, the *Inquirer* was purchased by the notoriously ruthless Moses Annenberg, who was imprisoned for tax evasion and died shortly after being released, in 1942, by which time his son Walter was running the paper and had softened its Republican orientation. The city's Democratic newspaper, the *Public Record*, went out of business in 1947, leaving only the *Inquirer*, the *Bulletin*, the African American *Philadelphia Tribune* (all of which endorsed the charter), the *Daily News* tabloid (which opposed the charter), and a variety of neighborhood newspapers. The reformers were certainly helped politically by the fact that Dilworth was the attorney for the *Inquirer* and close to both Moses and Walter Annenberg.[79]

The organizing and publicity efforts, newspaper endorsements, and steady stream of political scandals were the major ingredients leading to a large electoral victory in 1951: 65 percent of 399,915 voters approved the new city charter, a turnout roughly half that of the mayoral election later that year, which marked the most dramatic electoral realignment and the clearest reform cycle in the city's history. Democrats won every citywide office and fourteen out of seventeen city council seats. Joseph Clark was elected mayor (by a 58 percent majority), the first Democrat to do so since Samuel

King's election in 1881. Voters statewide also approved the city-county consolidation amendment, which, after much wrangling, allowed for the elimination of the elected Philadelphia county offices of recorder of deeds, coroner, inspectors of the board of county prisons, and city treasurer, the functions of which were absorbed into city offices. Yet, the sheriff, city commissioners, board of revision of taxes, registration commission, register of wills, and clerk of quarter sessions remained county offices outside city civil service rules.

While King's election in 1881 resulted from an ephemeral alliance between Democrats and reform Republicans, Clark's election reflected a deeper shift that had been building since the 1930s, in which the Republican Organization lost voters' allegiance through the declining significance of the tariff and the erosion of patronage through municipal unionization, an expanding civil service, and New Deal welfare and public works programs. A weakened GOP thus split into Meehan and Meade factions,[80] allowing independent Republican Thacher Longstreth to win the mayoral primary in 1955. Clark ran for U.S. Senate rather than for reelection, and Dilworth ran for mayor, beating Longstreth in the general election with a 59 percent majority.

With the possible exception of the period between the 1840s and the 1850s, the reform cycle that defined Philadelphia politics in the 1950s was, at least by the six criteria I described in the Introduction, the most sweeping and transformative in the history of the city: A clearly defined set of reformers was inspired by both new and old reform ideas regarding city charters, civil rights, and city planning; they brought together a broad coalition and decisively defeated a weakened and evidently corrupted political machine; and they fundamentally altered the city's developmental trajectory.

The 1951 charter reflected the Progressive Era belief in the ability of organizational changes to bring about political reform. It included several standard reform provisions in modified form. The new council consisted of ten members elected by district and seven elected at-large, with two at-large seats reserved for the minority party (held exclusively by Republicans from 1951 to 2019, when one seat was captured by the Working Families Party [WFP], discussed in Chapter 3). Instead of a city manager, the mayor appointed a managing director, who appointed and oversaw the heads of the main operational departments, a finance director, who appointed the heads of the collections and procurement departments, and a city representative, who also served as commerce director. The civil service was expanded to every city employee, except elected officers and a few of their direct appointees, and was overseen by a personnel director appointed by a civil service commission, whose three members were appointed by the mayor and chosen from nominees selected by a panel consisting of executives from Penn, Temple University, PBMR, the Chamber of Commerce, Philadelphia Fellowship Commission (PFC), American Federation of Labor, Central Labor Union, and the Congress of Industrial Organizations.[81]

The civil service nominating panel reflects the relative influence of major organizations at the time of the reform movement. The inclusion of the presidents of Temple University and Penn indicated the increasing importance of universities as they expanded dramatically after the war. The influx of returning veterans combined with generous education benefits provided through the 1944 GI Bill vastly expanded enrollments, campus expansions absorbed city streets and sometimes entire neighborhoods, and new federal funding for research added new laboratories and buildings.[82] The inclusion of the PFC—an interdenominational church–led umbrella organization founded in the 1930s in response to the rise of Fascism and racism during the Great Depression—reflected the increasing political importance of politics and civil rights. By 1951, the PFC was the city's primary civil rights organization and included "nine constituent agencies, a board of fifty-four, five hundred cooperating organizations, and five thousand individual members."[83]

Civil rights groups were part of the reform coalition, but the most influential members were the business-oriented groups who formed and fostered a broad network of actors and organizations. The city's business community was not necessarily unified around reform; many members of the Chamber of Commerce, especially, were hostile to Mayor Clark—yet, Clark and Dilworth were also corporate lawyers with strong business ties. The Chamber of Commerce and GPM also had somewhat divided memberships: The former more representative of the city's declining manufacturing sector and the latter more representative of professional service firms.[84] Yet, Chamber of Commerce presidents were regularly appointed to the GPM board, and, in 1954, PBMR merged into PEL.[85] These various groups were also closely intertwined with the ADA, whose thirty-two board members were "on probably every influential civic agency in town."[86] Philips, Clark, and Dilworth were all either founding or early members of both the ADA and the CPC; Clark was elected ADA chairman, in 1948, as was Dilworth, in 1949, and Philips, in 1962 and 1963. It was from these networks that Mayor Clark picked his cabinet—all of which had been CPC members—including Robert "Buck" Sawyer, a PBMR staff member who was hired by the Committee of Fifteen to work on its reports. Sawyer became the first GPM executive director, and then became the city's first managing director (the second GPM executive director, Donald Wagner, became managing director under Dilworth); Abraham Freedman, who had been in reform circles long enough to have worked on the 1943 Bullitt campaign, became city solicitor; Lennox Moak, a PEL staff member, became finance director; and Phillips became city representative and commerce director.

Political reform coincided with and partially defined the physical transformation of the city, fueled by new infusions of federal money through legislation related primarily to urban redevelopment, housing, and highways. "Center City," the downtown area defined by the 1682 street grid, was the primary focus for early redevelopment, promoted through the highly successful 1947 Better Philadelphia Exhibition, hosted at the Gimbel's downtown department store, the centerpiece of which was a scale model showing Center City with more parks and shopping plazas and ringed by expressways. Preparing the exhibition was the primary job of Bacon, who had joined the city planning commission after the war, was promoted as its executive director, in 1949, and reappointed to that position by Clark, in 1951 (and by the next two mayors as well).[87]

All of Center City was designated for land clearance and redevelopment, and, during the 1950s, construction began on three of the four expressways that would surround it on its eastern, western, and northern edges (a fourth expressway planned for the southern edge faced community resistance and was canceled in the 1970s).[88] The PRR demolished its massive Broad Street Station and accompanying elevated rail lines that cut through northwest Center City, thereby opening up more than twenty acres for redevelopment, which became the Penn Center plaza and office center. The National Park Service cleared land around Independence Hall for a large new park, connected by way of pedestrian "greenways" to the Society Hill neighborhood, which was itself to be gentrified through new housing, including three new thirty-story apartment buildings set in a park overlooking a marina, and the restoration of the neighborhood's impressive stock of colonial-era housing.[89]

These and other public works projects proceeded largely through the coordinated efforts of new quasi-governmental corporations, used, in part, to institutionalize the relationship between city government and business reform groups. The GPM, for instance, took a lead role in Society Hill by coordinating and managing the removal of a wholesale food market to a new Food Distribution Center in South Philadelphia and, then, by establishing with the city the Old Philadelphia Development Corporation (OPDC), to oversee redevelopment in the entire neighborhood and, later, over all of Center City. Similarly, the city and the Chamber of Commerce, along with major labor unions, partnered in the creation of the Philadelphia Industrial Development Corporation (PIDC), which helped locate and finance new sites and facilities for manufacturers in an effort to keep them from leaving the city.[90] (See Figure 2.6.)

Figure 2.6 "Ceremony for the start of redevelopment on Society Hill Houses," September 25, 1961. *From left to right:* Real estate developers William Zeckendorf and Albert Greenfield, Mayor Richardson Dilworth, and city council president James Tate. (Special Collections Research Center, Temple University Libraries, Philadelphia, PA.)

New and expanded federal programs funded both low-income public housing projects and new middle-income housing, built privately but subsidized through mortgages guaranteed by the Federal Housing Administration (FHA). FHA-backed mortgages stimulated housing demand and construction, especially in the city's northeastern neighborhoods and in surrounding counties, which, when combined with new expressways, fueled suburbanization. Thus, the population of neighboring Delaware County expanded by 78 percent between 1940 and 1960, while the city's population increased by a modest 7 percent during the 1940s (from 1.93 to 2.07 million) and then declined by 3 percent in the 1950s. And, as mostly white and middle-class residents left for the suburbs, businesses followed: In 1955, the city's largest private employer, Philco Radio and Television, moved out to neighboring Bucks County.[91]

One cause of suburbanization was the "white flight" of middle- and upper-middle-class residents away from the increasing number of Black people moving from Southern states as they escaped the brutality of Jim Crow and sharecropping and were attracted north by the promise of better jobs. The proportion of the city's population that was Black increased from 13 to 18 percent in the 1940s, then to 26 percent in 1960, and 34 percent in 1970.[92] A somewhat typical experience was that of Wilson Goode, the city's first Black mayor, whose sharecropping family moved from North Carolina when he was twelve, in 1954, and settled in Paschall, which Goode recollected as "an old, established, black, family neighborhood that lay nestled within the boundaries of a predominantly white ethnic enclave of southwest Philadelphia . . . it stuck out like a sore thumb, a black island in the midst of a white oasis." Despite going to an integrated school and having white friends, Goode found that "coming to Philadelphia had made no real difference in my life. The racial barriers were just as strong here as they'd been down South."[93]

The new arrivals found themselves constrained to living in existing Black neighborhoods, prohibited from living elsewhere by racist realtor and bank lending practices (reinforced by FHA guidelines) and the open hostility of white residents. Public housing was also segregated and in short supply. Yet, the sheer increase in the number of Black residents meant that they were compelled to look for new places to live, often facing violent crowds, especially in select white working-class neighborhoods, and triggering white exoduses through realtor "block busting" practices. Many of the city's largest private employers hired no Black people until the late 1930s, they were typically restricted to the lowest positions, and, as the city lost manufacturing jobs after World War II, they were the first to be laid off.[94] Thus, by 1959, "black men and women accounted for 43 percent of the city's unemployed." Most unions resisted integration, one exception being the DC 33 municipal workers, where Black Philadelphians found some of the easiest employment paths, in large part because of stronger civil service rules.[95]

Dilworth, Clark, and other reformers and Democrats were ideologically committed to civil rights and also saw the electoral advantages Black support might provide. They allied with the city's Black politicians and advocacy groups and supported the establishment of a city-level Fair Employment Practices Committee that could investigate and issue fines for discriminatory hiring practices. Republicans were strategically and ideologically divided, but, in 1948, in a move considered a victory by most of the city's civil rights groups, a majority of city council members, all of whom were Republicans, voted in favor of a weak version of the Fair Employment Practices Committee with investigatory but not regulatory authority.[96] The commission was made a permanent agency with expanded authority by the 1951 charter and renamed the Commission on Human Relations (CHR).[97] Its connection to the reform movement is suggested by the fact that the first CHR commissioner was an ADA activist from Detroit, George Schermer.[98]

Foretelling a future electoral split, Dilworth and Clark both won their respective offices in 1951 with more than 60 percent of the Black vote, an even higher percentage of the Jewish vote, but less than 50 percent of the Irish and Italian vote,[99] though they also performed well in the rapidly growing and overwhelmingly white wards of the Northeast—something that would be less true of future Democrats.[100] When Dilworth became mayor, he formally recognized AFSCME as "the exclusive bargaining agent for all nonuniformed personnel" while simultaneously initiating a stealth voter registration drive in the Streets Department so as to sign up new Black Democrats.[101]

By the time of Dilworth's mayoralty, the Democratic Party was reestablishing itself as a machine-style organization. City committee chairman and city council president James Finnegan had been supportive of the reform movement, but he had left both positions by 1955 and was replaced as committee chair by Congressman William J. Green, who consistently pressed both Clark and Dilworth for patronage and attempted to amend the charter to exempt more city jobs from the civil service. The amendment failed but Green was accommodated by Dilworth, who needed the party's support to win both the mayoralty and the governorship, for which he ran unsuccessfully in 1962. Dilworth's acquiescence to the party alienated reformers, most notably those in the ADA, which was, by the 1960s, losing power and influence.[102]

The charter specified that city officials had to resign their elected positions before running for another office, and, thus, Dilworth resigned in 1962 to run for governor. Council president James Tate became mayor, signaling the eclipse of the reform movement and the rise of the Democratic organization. Green died in 1963 and reformers attempted to retake the Democratic Party, running Walter Phillips in the mayoral primary, in which he captured less than 30 percent of the vote. Tate was unable to construct the kind of powerful machine that the Republicans had had earlier in the century, in part because of the new civil service protections provided by the new charter. In addition, quasi-public and semi-independent corporations such as PIDC were able to resist attempts to use them as patronage outposts. For this reason, but also because of his uniquely caustic personality, Tate alienated much of the city's political establishment, including the wards, but maintained a fragile coalition consisting largely of Black and union voters.[103]

A Democratic Machine, the Urban Crisis, and Two-Party Competition

Defining Philadelphia politics from the 1960s through the 1980s were race, Rizzo, increasingly powerful and politically active unions, and a semblance of two-party competition. Whereas Democratic reform mayoral candidates had been winning general elections by steadily increasing proportions—from 58, to 59, to 65 percent in 1951, 1955, and 1959, respectively—Tate won against Republican candidate James McDermott in 1963 with 55 percent of the vote. And whereas the city council in 1959 consisted of fifteen Democrats and two Republicans (who held the two at-large minority party seats), Republicans also won two district seats in 1963. In 1967, Tate won against former DA and GOP candidate Arlen Specter with a plurality of only 49 percent; Specter won 47 percent, with the remainder split among three third-party candidates.

One of the third-party candidates was Cecil B. Moore, who, in 1963, was elected president of the Philadelphia branch of the National Association for the Advancement of Colored People (NAACP). Moore's election represented a distinct break from the traditionally conservative leadership of the NAACP, which had historically functioned much like the white reformer social clubs of the nineteenth century. Moore led protests and sit-ins to integrate the building trades unions and institutions such as Girard College, a boarding school founded in 1848 with admission reserved, per banker Stephen Girard's will, for "poor white male orphans." He likened himself to a traditional political boss concerned with jobs and railed against the political ineffectiveness of middle- and upper-middle-class Black people. He was effective but divisive and was run out of the NAACP leadership in 1966. His 1967 mayoral campaign was idiosyncratic, but, in a reflection of reform strategies from earlier in the twentieth century, he was not the last major Black political figure to run for mayor on a third-party ticket.[104]

The two council districts captured by Republicans in 1963 comprised nearly the entirety of the vast and rapidly growing Northeast, home of GOP boss Meehan's Thirty-Fifth Ward. The area attracted approximately one hundred thousand new residents in the 1950s, mostly to new suburban-style homes financed with FHA-backed mortgages, and was overwhelmingly white and working class, with factories that employed approximately 20 percent of Philadelphia's industrial workforce. Efforts to integrate the area by the CHR were strongly opposed by residents and groups such as the Philadelphia Northeast Realty Board. Large expanses of South Philadelphia were also vigorous in maintaining their whiteness in the 1960s and 1970s, in large part by blocking proposed public housing projects.[105]

South and Northeast Philadelphia became bastions of Nixon's "silent majority" and later "Reagan Democrats": Republicans and conservative Democrats who rallied around "law and order" candidates such as Specter and later Frank Rizzo, who started the 1960s as a police inspector and ended the decade as police commissioner, becoming famous for such things as raiding hippie coffeehouses and the headquarters of Black activist groups and allegedly giving the command to police to "beat their black asses," regarding student protestors at a large rally at school district headquarters in 1967. "Rizzocrat" voters were driven politically by their resistance to neighborhood, workplace, and school integration and by a sense of increasing disorder, driven by rising crime rates and events such as the 1964 race riot in North Philadelphia, which received extra salience with the rise of local television news coverage. They were increasingly alienated by liberals such as Dilworth, who after his failed gubernatorial bid was appointed president of the school board and, with school superintendent Mark Shedd, led an aggressive campaign of integration and student empowerment.[106]

On the other side of the political spectrum were the civil rights groups that had been part of the 1950s reform coalition, such as the PFC, and an increasing number of groups frustrated by the limited impact of the CHR and who pursued more confrontational strategies, such as the protests led by the NAACP under Moore, and the 400 Ministers, a coalition of Black church leaders who led boycotts against companies that resisted integrating their workforces. Leon Sullivan, a minister and leader of the boycott movement, founded the influential Opportunities Industrialization Center (OIC), in 1964, which provided technical training to Black Philadelphians, in part to circumvent the deeply segregated building trades unions' apprenticeship programs.[107] A similar effort was the Philadelphia Urban Coalition (PUC, later renamed the Urban Affairs Coalition); established in 1969 as a "loose coalition of community, business, political, and labor representatives," it vaguely resembled both the GPM and public-private partnerships, such as PIDC, but focused on strategies to help integrate the city's workforce.[108]

Both the OIC and PUC were supported by local business leaders, the Chamber of Commerce, and the GPM,[109] though these groups had receded from local politics. As historian Guian McKee notes, "The decline of Philadelphia as a corporate headquarters location reduced the pool of talent available to replace these leaders, and as a result, it remained uncertain whether such uncompleted, large-scale public-private projects as the Market East Mall in Center City or the University City Science Center in West Philadelphia would receive the cohesive elite political support that had once been provided for the Food Distribution Center, Society Hill, and even PIDC."[110] Similarly, PEL, the Committee of Seventy, CCCP, and the CPC continued throughout the 1960s and into the 1970s but retreated into their specific policy niches and their secondary roles as social clubs.

The increasing divisiveness of civil rights, race, and integration left Mayor Tate astraddle hostile factions of white working-class and Black voters for his 1967 reelection bid. Two of his key allies in doing so were Samuel Evans, a Black power broker who had been involved in local politics and civil rights activism since the 1930s, and Charles Bowser, a Black attorney and civil rights activist. With his access to patronage limited by civil service rules and municipal unions, Tate tapped money available through the federal community action programs, part of the Johnson administration's War on Poverty, authorized by Congress in 1964 and administered by the federal Office of Economic Opportunity (OEO). To distribute community action money and "counteract an alliance of reform Democrats and ward leaders," Evans designed the Philadelphia Anti-Poverty Action Committee, and Tate appointed Bowser its executive director (he would later serve as a deputy mayor under Tate and then as PUC's executive director). The Philadelphia Anti-Poverty Action Committee's board included "civil rights leaders, representatives of business, labor, and social service organizations . . . and a sufficient number of actual poor people to satisfy OEO's demands for community participation" but was structured to maintain the mayor's control; its success is reflected in the fact that Tate captured an average of 66 percent of the vote in the city's majority Black wards, as opposed to 43 percent of the vote in the white wards, in 1967.[111]

The other key pillar in Tate's electoral strategy was to gain the support of organized labor. Municipal unions had become more aggressive in their negotiations with the city over wages and benefits and their threats of strikes. The city's teachers unionized in 1965; white-collar employees organized into AFSCME DC 47; and the Fraternal Order of Police lodge, formed in the 1940s, became far more vocal in supporting conservative law-and-order positions. The locals comprising DC 33 almost split along racial lines over contract disputes, part of the resolution to which was that DC 33 president Bill McEntee was replaced as chief negotiator by sanitation workers head Earl Stout, who hailed from an old and prominent Black Republican family, his father having served as sheriff prior to World War II. Stout successfully bargained for the most generous package offered to municipal blue-collar workers in the history of the city (police and firefighters got equally generous contracts) leading former city finance director Lennox Moak, who had returned to PEL as its director, to comment that "such liberality with the public purse is without precedent in any major city in the United States." Yet, it worked for Tate, who received DC 33's first-ever mayoral endorsement and whose members actively campaigned on his behalf. In exchange, Stout gained control over the operations of the Streets Department's sanitation division.[112]

Another powerful labor faction was the building trades unions (plumbers, roofers, ironworkers, electricians, sheet metal workers, steamfitters, and elevator constructors), representing approximately nine thousand of the highest-paid blue-collar workers in the region. Much of the building trades' political cohesion and activism came from their resistance to integration. Partially in response to protests by the NAACP and Congress on Racial Equality over the lack of skilled Black workers at city government work sites, both city and federal agencies instituted minority hiring requirements for building contracts, known as the "Philadelphia Plan." The plans led to marginal increases in the number of Black workers in the building trades but also made the unions—most notably Local 98 of the International Brotherhood of Electrical Workers—more politically active and further divided the labor and civil rights wings of the local Democratic-reform coalition.[113]

Tate supported the Philadelphia Plan,[114] but, to shore up his support among blue-collar white people, he disbanded the police review board that had been established during the 1950s and, for the 1967 election, made a show of promising to maintain Rizzo as police commissioner. Rizzo had astutely used the media and his leadership positions in the police to set himself up as a viable mayoral candidate in 1971. Running almost entirely on his appeal to white working-class voters in South and Northeast Philadelphia, Rizzo's election in 1971 was the closest thing to a Republican realignment away from the Democrats that the city had seen since the 1850s. Rizzo had been a lifelong Republican and campaigned on a platform, that, to the extent it had any substance, was largely indistinguishable from that of his ally Richard Nixon, yet, for the purposes of winning the mayoral election had switched his affiliation and run as a Democrat. And Rizzo's victory in the Democratic primary, by a plurality of 49 percent, was made possible, in part, by the fact that some twenty thousand Republicans in the city switched parties so that they could vote for him.[115]

Thacher Longstreth, who, since losing to Dilworth in 1964, had become the Chamber of Commerce vice president and an at-large council member, won the Republican primary, and the general election was, thus, defined by a Democratic candidate who looked more like a Republican, supported by the building trades, and a Republican candidate who looked more like a Democrat, who was endorsed by Dilworth, Clark, the GPM, and who captured the vast majority of the Black vote.[116] Rizzo's victory in 1971 was also, in part, a result of a split between mostly white business-oriented reformers and the city's Black political leadership, reflected in the Democratic primary by the fact that a white reform-oriented candidate, William Green III (son of the former Democratic city chairman), competed against a Black reform candidate, state representative Hardy Williams. The combined votes for Williams and Green were only 3,693 less (out of 361,509 votes for all primary candidates) than those cast for Rizzo.

Williams's campaign was supported by the BPF, founded in 1968 by younger Black politicians and activists to target the Democratic Party for greater racial representation. As such, BPF was similar to earlier reform organizations such as the Municipal League in using "the very electoral organizing skills that made the . . . ward organizations so effective."[117] Another founding BPF member was Williams's campaign manager, Wilson Goode, at the time executive director of a Ford Foundation–funded community services organization, where he was building political connections, community ties, and a reputation as a competent manager.

Rizzo's outsize personality and media presence (several friendly journalists got jobs in his administration), and his ability to develop patronage resources (especially in the public authorities that were not subject to city civil service rules) and thus build his own organization outside of the Democratic Party, made him the city's defining political figure in the 1970s.[118] (See Figure 2.7.) Yet, several other factors significantly shaped Philadelphia politics in that decade, most notably the mass exodus from the city. During the two decades between 1950 and 1970, Philadelphia suffered a net population loss of 123,000 people; during the 1970s alone, the city lost slightly more than 260,000 people, or 13 percent of its population.

There were multiple causes for Philadelphia's precipitous decline. A 1974 Supreme Court ruling that integration plans were required within but not across school districts incentivized white flight and furthered de facto racial segregation between cities and suburbs. Population and job loss became self-reinforcing processes; during Tate's second term (1968–1972) the city lost "724 industrial firms and 61,300 manufacturing jobs."[119] During Rizzo's mayoralty, the city lost 138,814 jobs, 77,600 of which were in manufacturing. Between 1970 and 1980, unemployment rose from 4.6 to 11.2 percent, and the percentage of the city's population on welfare rose from 14 to 20 percent. The combination of racialized poverty, segregation, crime, and television came together in the popularization of the idea of an "urban underclass," used to describe neighborhoods such as North Philadelphia—known since the 1960s as "The Jungle." As described in a 1977 *Time* magazine cover story, such neighborhoods produced "the nation's juvenile delinquents, school

Figure 2.7 "Plans for a new garment center are discussed at 3 Girard Plaza by (*from left*) Stephen S. Gardner, chairman of the Greater Philadelphia Movement; William Ross, manager of the Philadelphia Dress Joint Board of the International Ladies Garment Workers' Union, and Mayor Rizzo," June 29, 1973. (Special Collections Research Center, Temple University Libraries, Philadelphia, PA.)

dropouts, drug addicts and welfare mothers, and much of the adult crime, family disruption, urban decay and demand for social expenditures."[120] Images of the urban underclass were broadcast on the nightly news through the televisions that were in practically every American home (a phenomenon only twenty years old at that point), making major cities such as Philadelphia distinctly unattractive places to move or even visit.

As Philadelphia's economy contracted, municipal unions increased in power, especially after Stout—who quickly became a Rizzo ally—was elected DC 33's president in 1974. After the union supported his reelection, Rizzo offered DC 33 a generous contract, including an agreement to "discontinue management review of worker performance, effectively conceding power of the Streets Department to the union." As union strength led to better contract negotiations, the city was compelled to raise wage and property taxes and water and sewer fees. The wage tax, established in 1939 and paid by both

Figure 2.8 "Philadelphia Party mayoral candidate Charles W. Bowser (*right*) is greeted by Peter J. Camiel, Democratic Party chairman, at last night's Democratic fundraising dinner. Gov. Shapp is next to Camiel, while Sen. John Durkin is beside Shapp," October 28, 1975. (Special Collections Research Center, Temple University Libraries, Philadelphia, PA.)

city residents and suburban residents who worked in the city, increased from 2 to 4.3 percent, in 1976, and to 4.96 percent, in 1984.[121]

The 1975 city elections once again reflected separate coalitions of Black politicians, traditional liberal reformers, and conservative white working-class voters. Rizzo's challenger in the Democratic mayoral primary was Louis Hill, a state legislator and Dilworth's stepson, who captured only 43 percent of the vote. In a classic reform move, Tate ally and former Urban Affairs Coalition president Charles Bowser ran in the general election as a BPF-backed candidate on the "Philadelphia Party" ticket, performed notably well in the city's "white reform wards," and won 25 percent of the vote, beating Republican Tom Foglietta, who won only 18 percent.[122] (See Figure 2.8.)

Rizzo's second term started with revelations of an $86 million city budget deficit, announcements of wage tax increases, city worker layoffs that sparked a sanitation slowdown, a bicentennial celebration generally considered an expensive failure, and plans to close the city's general hospital, all of which brought together what remained of the traditional reform groups, such as the Committee of Seventy, the ADA, and GPM (renamed the Greater Philadelphia Partnership), with Black political leadership, in a "recall Rizzo" movement, calling for new elections. The Pennsylvania Supreme Court ruled the recall unconstitutional but the reform coalition it brought together was rejuvenated when Rizzo attempted to change the charter so that he could run for a third consecutive term. The proposed charter change was included on the ballot in the 1978 elections, which had the effect of increasing the Black proportion of registered voters from 32 to 38 percent, thereby increasing the potential for getting a Black mayor elected in 1979.[123]

Bowser ran for mayor again in 1979, this time in the Democratic primary against Green. He won majorities in all of the city's majority-Black wards, but not by enough, and Green won by 53 percent of the votes. In the general election, Republican candidate David Marston pledged to appoint a Black managing director and Green promised to do the same, thereby gaining endorsements from several prominent Black politicians, including Bowser. There was once again a Black third-party candidate, councilman Lucien Blackwell, president of the longshoreman's union, Stout ally, and a more patronage-oriented politician. Green was elected mayor in 1979 with 53 percent of the vote, compared to 30 percent for Marston and 18 percent for Blackwell.[124]

Political scientist Richard Keiser has argued that the substantial support Green got in the general election from Black voters was somewhat distinct to Philadelphia, where there was at least the potential for a biracial civil rights–reform coalition—brought together by their mutual distaste for Rizzo but also by the long-standing support for civil rights among white reformers—which provided Black reform-oriented politicians the latitude to support white reform-oriented mayoral candidates. By contrast, in Chicago where there had been no substantial postwar reform cycle, "Blacks who considered supporting white reformers were castigated as Uncle Toms who were selling out to another plantation master."[125]

Green appointed Wilson Goode managing director, and, in response, Stout promised a work slowdown since his ally Orville Jones had not been appointed. The image of DC 33's president appearing to believe he could control mayoral appointments led to a wave of negative publicity that, combined with an *Inquirer* exposé of corrupt practices in the union (prompted by an ultimately fruitless federal investigation), reinforced Stout's image as a traditional political boss.[126] The negative press provided Mayor Green some political leverage to bargain for union concessions as the city "faced a $167 million deficit and a declining bond rating" in his first year in office, in part from declining federal funds and also from a 10 percent wage increase granted to DC 33 in the final year of the Rizzo administration.[127] Union members were provided a 10 percent wage hike during the second year of the Green administration, but there were simultaneous layoffs and the early 1980s were still defined by municipal labor strife, including a fifty-day teachers' strike in response to layoffs, in 1981, and an eighty-day transit workers' strike, in 1983.

The investigations into DC 33 followed the broader trend of federal law enforcement investigating and prosecuting state and local corruption, pioneered by the U.S. attorney for Western Pennsylvania, Richard Thornburgh, who was promoted to assistant attorney general for the Department of Justice's criminal division, in 1975, and then elected Pennsylvania's governor, in 1979. Other early federal investigations into corruption in Philadelphia were the "Abscam" case that led to the indictment of three city council members in 1980, and, also in 1980, the indictment of Vincent Fumo, a newly elected state senator and rising star in the Democratic machine, on mail fraud charges related to "no show" patronage jobs on the state payroll (Fumo was convicted but acquitted shortly thereafter; Stout was ultimately indicted and convicted in 1988 on charges stemming from a later investigation).[128]

In 1983, Green declined to run for a second term, and both Goode and Rizzo ran in the Democratic primary along with several other candidates. Goode won the primary with 53 percent of the vote (compared to 43 percent for Rizzo) and then went on to win the general election—which, for only the second time since 1967, did not include a third-party Black candidate—with 55 percent of the vote. A large part of Goode's electoral success was the coalition he put together of Black voters, liberal reformers, and even a good portion of labor—he was endorsed by DC 33, DC 47, and the Local 1199 hospital workers—though he did not see unions as "critical to his political fortune."[129] He could combine his community activist background with an image as a technocratic, business-friendly reformer who was a long-standing ADA member and a recipient of the Chamber of Commerce's "outstanding young leader" award and who had cut costs during his time as chair of the Pennsylvania Public Utility Commission.

Like reformers earlier in the century, "Goode formed a task force drawn from the regional business community to advise him in hiring only the most qualified officers for city supervisory and management positions, announcing that he intended to run the city like a Fortune 500 company."[130] Yet, Goode's business community support faded, first after the catastrophic 1985 MOVE bombing, when the city's effort to remove a back-to-nature cult from their West Philadelphia residence resulted in eleven deaths and sixty-one destroyed homes. Unlike Rizzo and Tate, Goode took a hard line in union negotiations, leading to long strikes by both DC 33 and DC 47. The mayor's inability to work with the city council meant that several initiatives, including cable television service, a trash incinerator, and a convention center, languished (though the convention center was ultimately built). And, finally, the Goode administration suffered from an increasing fiscal crisis, as people and businesses continued to leave—the city lost "13 percent of its middle class residents" during the 1980s and thirty-five thousand jobs in 1988 and 1989 alone—and federal aid to Philadelphia declined from $250 million to just $54 million during the decade.[131]

At the same time, Goode ended up using the municipal strikes to his advantage. He seriously and publicly considered privatizing city sanitation services, which provided him with leverage in union negotiations and made him look tough on what was perceived to be one of the pillars of the city political machine. In response, DC 33 endorsed Rizzo, who, in 1987, ran for mayor as a Republican, where he handily won the primary. Rizzo's move to the GOP made some sense given his ideology and temperament, but it was also strategic; the former mayor saw that white people were defecting to the Republican Party. Between 1983 and 1990, the percentage of registered Democrats in the city who were white declined from 54 to 42 percent and the number of registered Democrats overall declined by two hundred thousand while Republicans increased by sixty-two thousand. By 1990, the proportion of Democrats among the city's registered voters was still high at 72 percent, but the lowest it had been since 1973.[132] The surprise election of Republican Ron Castille as DA, in 1985, also made it clear that many city Democrats were willing to vote for a GOP candidate.

In contrast to his 55 percent majority in 1983, Goode beat Rizzo with only 51 percent of the vote in 1987. The percent of white people who voted for Goode was estimated to have declined from 23 to 20 percent between 1983 and 1987 while in both elections he won approximately 97 percent of the Black vote.[133] The mayor had overperformed in white liberal upper-class neighborhoods of Center City and Northwest Philadelphia in both 1983 and 1987, but, by 1990, one Democratic political strategist noted, "The superliberal white faction, the people any black candidate needs, are most disappointed by Goode's performance." In fact, by the end of his mayoralty, a "private Democratic poll," in 1989, found that "Goode was viewed unfavorably by 66 percent of all voters surveyed; only 23 percent gave favorable marks. Even black Democratic committeemen report antipathy toward Goode in their own neighborhoods."[134]

Both Goode, in the 1980s, and Blankenburg, in the 1910s, had campaigned on business-friendly reform platforms but faced opposition among the city's power brokers and were generally considered ineffectual. Yet, only Blankenburg is remembered as a reformer. There are at least three key differences. First, Blankenburg was mayor during an era when reform was a salient and popular idea and slogan; Goode was mayor during an era when the prevalent ideology was best captured by Ronald Reagan's famous 1981 quote that "gov-

Figure 2.9 "Meeting in city council chambers," April 13, 1980. Seated in front are DA Edward Rendell and deputy mayor Wilson Goode. Goode and Rendell served successively as mayor, from 1984 to 1992 and 1992 to 2000, respectively. (Special Collections Research Center, Temple University Libraries, Philadelphia, PA.)

ernment is not a solution to our problem; government is the problem." Second, Blankenburg was mayor in a growing and economically vibrant city that represented "progress"; Goode was mayor of a declining city in a suburbanizing country. Third, Goode was Black, and, in the simplistic story lines that dominated television coverage, Black politicians were represented more than their white counterparts as appealing to special interests rather than the interests of the whole community.[135] Goode was thus depicted as a Black person rather than as a reform candidate, and one that had alienated white people from the Democratic Party. (See Figure 2.9.)

Rendell as a Reform Mayor

With a municipal bond rating near junk level, the city attempted a $375 million tax anticipation note (a short-term bond) in 1990, and failed, bringing negative national publicity and underscoring the fact that the mayor elected in 1991 would face a massive municipal deficit. Federal assistance declined even as the city faced the AIDS and crack cocaine epidemics and crime rates increased. Philadelphia lost one hundred thousand people in the 1980s and the number of jobs declined by 5 percent; in 1991, the Naval Shipyard closed, "eliminating over 5,000 well-paying, skilled trade jobs."[136] The poverty rate had remained at roughly 20 percent through the 1980s, well above the average for the country overall and concentrated in mostly Black neighborhoods.

As media scholar Phyllis Kaniss noted with regard to the 1991 mayoral election, it was one "in which the problems of the city had never been more complex but in which the themes of media coverage would never be simpler."[137] Over the 1980s, the city's media landscape had changed significantly. The *Bulletin*, founded in 1847 and once the city's highest-circulation paper, closed in 1982, leaving just the *Inquirer, Daily News*, and *Tribune*. Newspapers competed with the local television news, but the city's population loss and decline forced all media outlets to focus on stories that were more attractive to suburbanites, with limited city election coverage that focused on dramatic story lines and caricatures rather than policy issues.[138]

The Republican primary featured Rizzo, who had maintained his public profile with a radio talk show, former DA and presumed front-runner Ron Castille, and municipal financial consultant Sam Katz, cast as the technocrat. Castille faced an onslaught of unsubstantiated accusations from Rizzo about his drinking and mental health while Katz gained substantial positive media exposure but remained a second-tier candidate, occasionally suspected of allying with Rizzo to take votes from Castille. Katz won 28 percent of the primary vote while Rizzo beat Castille in an upset victory by 1,429 votes.[139]

The main contenders in the Democratic primary were Ed Rendell, a former DA who had run unsuccessfully in the Democratic primaries for governor, in 1986, and mayor, in 1987, and two Black candidates, Lucien Blackwell and George Burrell. Blackwell had served on the city council for twenty years and as previously noted had run for mayor on a third-party ticket in 1979. Burrell was an attorney who had worked for elite law firms, was a deputy mayor in the Green administration, and then was elected to city council where he "had taken the 'good government' positions against the powerful ruling clique of fellow black councilmen," namely Blackwell, John Street, and council president Joe Coleman. Perhaps most important, Burrell had the backing of William Gray III, one of the most powerful Democrats in the U.S. House (to which he had been elected in 1978) and a founder of the coalition of Black Philadelphia politicians known as the Northwest Alliance, a successor to the BPF. Throughout the campaign Burrell battled rumors that he was simply running at the behest of Gray, who did not want Blackwell to be mayor.[140]

Rendell won the primary with 49 percent of the vote while Blackwell and Burrell won 27 and 15 percent, respectively. Rizzo died shortly after the primaries and the Republican City Committee under the direction of "boss" Bill Meehan (son of former boss Austin Meehan) selected as its replacement candidate former PIDC director John Egan, who captured slightly more than

30 percent of the vote in the general election. As a reflection of the state of the city's GOP, the choice of a relatively weak and unknown mayoral candidate was often presumed to be a desire on the part of the Republicans to lose the election so as to not jeopardize patronage jobs provided by the Democrats.[141]

The 1991 mayoral election could hardly be counted as a reform victory. In contrast to an election such as the one in 1947 when reformers excited voters and increased turnout, in 1991, turnout in both the primaries and the general election reached record lows (it would decrease even further in future elections).[142] There were no third-party reform candidates, the Democratic primary indicated a continued split between white and Black voters and political coalitions, and the candidates in both primaries who seemed to best fit the mold of reformer (Burrell and Katz) both came in third place. Finally, the winner, Rendell, gave "no indication that he plan[ned] to govern as a reformer and root out patronage, corruption, or abuse of power . . . although he heads a biracial coalition that continues to advance Black empowerment, it is not reformist like its predecessors."[143] As mayor, Rendell worked within the Democratic Party and with power brokers such as state senator Vincent Fumo and council president John Street, and he was dismissive of reform hobbyhorses such as city planning or campaign finance reform.

Yet, if Rendell was not interested in reform, he found himself mayor in a context that practically required it of him—in stark contrast to Goode, a reformer in the absence of the conditions necessary for reform, especially for a Black mayor. The early 1990s were marked by the first Democratic presidential administration since the 1970s, one that was inspired by the idea of "reinventing government"—the title of what has been credited as the most influential book on government reform in the past thirty years, published in 1992, which argued that "government managers and employees could and should . . . be as entrepreneurial as their private-sector counterparts. This meant embracing competition; measuring outcomes rather than inputs or processes; and insisting on accountability."[144] Rendell was held out by the newly elected Clinton administration as a national model of this kind of reform—Vice President Al Gore famously called him "America's Mayor"—praised for his successes in downtown development, attracting state and federal money, challenging the unions, eliminating the deficit and creating budget surpluses, raising the city's bond rating, promoting privatization and performance management, and, along with DA Lynne Abraham, pushing a "law and order" policy regarding policing and sentencing that did not alienate progressive voters.[145]

Though specific policy prescriptions differed, the general themes of efficiency and accountability in reinventing government were the same as those that inspired reformers in the early twentieth century. And, faced with a $250 million deficit, Rendell laid out the equivalent of a reform-based plan, including the establishment of an Office of Management and Productivity. He sought to reconstruct some semblance of the GPM by establishing a "volunteer task force of three hundred executives to introduce the types of efficiency standards that were the byline in the private sector." Similar to Goode, he took a hard line with municipal unions, resulting in a reform-machine political fight in all but name. Similar to the exposés of government waste and corruption by reformers in the 1950s, the Rendell administration exposed union corruption such as overtime abuses among city workers and offered DC 33 a contract that included a wage freeze for more than two years and significant reductions in benefits. The contract prompted a short strike, but, with little political or public support, the unions agreed to the concessions in less than a day.[146]

And, even as Rendell was dismissive of planning, he promoted and sold a new image of the city's downtown, similar to what Ed Bacon had done with the Better Philadelphia Exhibition. Instead of the expressways and greenways that reflected progress in the 1940s and 1950s, in the 1990s, the focus was on arts and culture, entertainment, and a vibrant street life, marked by projects such as a new convention center, a new park and museum at Independence Hall, and rebranding South Broad Street as the "Avenue of the Arts" with a new music hall—many of which had begun well before Rendell, but his administration organized these projects into a cohesive plan that recognized the emergent importance of the tourism and downtown service industries. There was a clear organizational connection between downtown revitalization projects in the 1950s and 1990s as well, as the original OPDC— the partnership between the city and the GPM that had been instrumental in such things as the Food Distribution Center—became the Center City District in 1990, a business improvement district that provided extra security services and street cleaning to promote downtown businesses and that has more recently spearheaded and managed such projects as the reconstruction of Dilworth Park next to city hall and a new rail park immediately north of downtown.

In short, Rendell's election and mayoral administration represent a reform cycle in the sense that it was inspired by new ideas regarding the city, and, in successfully implementing those ideas against a "machine" of ostensibly rent-seeking municipal unions, it in some respects fundamentally transformed how the city functioned. Yet, the 1990s differed from previous reform eras in Philadelphia possibly most notably in the failure of a new charter commission, established by the city council in 1992. Through the first half of the twentieth century and culminating in 1951, charters were seen as fundamental to reforming the city, through such things as a stronger civil service and remaking the mayor as a corporate executive. Charter reform, in 1951, involved mass mobilization through a broad-based movement involving a dense network of groups, influential business organizations, and extensive promotion in the press. In 1992, by contrast, the longstanding director of the increasingly ineffectual Committee of Seventy, Fred Voight, was friends with Rendell and had suggested the idea of a charter commission. The commission quickly became embroiled in a power struggle, with council president Street appointing himself chair, leading city controller Jonathan Saidel to actively campaign against the commission's proposed charter revisions. Rather than the sweeping reforms proposed in previous charters, the 1992 commission came up with sixty recommendations that covered minutiae such as shifting the responsibility for numbering contracts from the director of finance to the Law Department. When included on the ballot in the 1994 primary elections, the commission's recommendations were rejected by an overwhelming vote.[147]

In a city with a weaker business community that was poorer, still shrinking, and more racially divided, with declining voter turnout and a contracting local press, reform was driven not by mass movements but in response to crises and by technocrats. Yet, at the same time, there were clear continuities between the 1990s and previous reform eras, such as that between the OPDC and the Center City District, and the persistence of groups such as the Committee of Seventy and PEL, even as they did not play major roles as they had in the past. The constant threat of Rizzo also lent continuity to reform efforts; after he won the 1991 Republican primary, a sizable constituency from the 1976 Citizens Committee to Recall Rizzo volunteered for Rendell, and former ADA director Rich Chapman "took charge of field operations for the Rendell campaign."[148] And, finally, though not particularly related to reform, the 1991 city council elections saw an unusually high level of turnover with the election of seven new members—two of which, Michael Nutter and James Kenney, would later become mayors.

PAST AND PRESENT PROGRESSIVE ERAS AND
THE FUTURE OF PHILADELPHIA POLITICS

Philadelphia is marked by a contemporary progressive movement similar to that of the early twentieth century. Comparing the two eras provides the basis for speculating about the city's future politics. The new
progressive agenda revolves around equity and redistribution and is pursued
by newer groups such as Reclaim Philadelphia and the Working Families Party (WFP), who have scored electoral victories in the wards, state legislature,
and city council. It overlaps with but also conflicts at various points with the
agendas of good-government, urbanist reformers, represented by long-standing groups such as the Committee of Seventy but also by newer groups such
as Philadelphia 3.0 ("3.0").

All of these groups operate in a city that has changed dramatically but
is just as monolithically Democratic as it was monolithically Republican one
hundred years ago, creating the same pressures to reform the dominant party through intraparty factions and third parties—thus the WFP is similar to
the third parties of the 1900s. In a one-party town, the distinction between
"machine" and "reform" becomes blurred; reform is typically halting and
incremental and proceeds, in part, through ephemeral third parties, just as it
did a century earlier. This is in contrast to the 1950s, when a reform cycle combined with a party realignment led to more sweeping changes such as the
1951 city charter.

The progressive coalition of the early twentieth century fragmented and
collapsed back into the Republican Organization by the 1920s. The contemporary Democratic "machine" is weak and fragmented compared to the Vare-

Penrose machine, and, thus, to the extent that the contemporary progressive coalition breaks apart, there is less of an organization into which it might be reabsorbed, which will lead to a more fragmented and directionless politics. At least three other trends also encourage greater fragmentation: Persistent economic inequality, a weaker press fragmented among niche news providers, and historically low voter turnout. My vision of an increasingly politically fragmented future city is hopefully qualified by Philadelphia's economic resurgence, which holds out some hope that decentralization might lead to a more robustly democratic system capable of innovative policies.

My story of Philadelphia's future politics begins with the election of John Street, in 1999, whose administration embodied both the seeds of contemporary progressivism and some flagrant elements of machine-style politics, highlighted by FBI investigations. Two related responses to perceived (and real) corruption were new and consequential campaign finance rules adopted in 2005 and the 2007 election of a classic good-government reformer, Michael Nutter. The context for Nutter's mayoralty was the Great Recession but also an economic resurgence concentrated in and around Center City even as citywide family incomes remained low and unemployment and poverty remained persistently high. Issues of inequality and equity combined with local activism defined a new progressive political movement that helped council member James Kenney get elected mayor in 2015. More than Kenney's election, however, the 2016 presidential election spurred liberal activism, empowered by and empowering the new progressive coalition, which when combined with recent successes by more traditional good-government reformers suggests that a new reform cycle has opened up a new chapter in the city's politics.

Politics as Usual with Mayor John Street

During the 1990s, Philadelphia lost 68,027 people and 61,600 jobs, household incomes declined by 7 percent, and poverty increased by 2.6 percent. Economic inequality also rose: As proportions of the city population, families making less than $34,000 annually (in USD [2000]) increased by 5 percent, those making more than $81,000 also increased, though by less than 1 percent, while those with middle incomes declined by 11 percent. The city became more racially segregated but also more diverse: The white population declined overall and in select outlying neighborhoods but increased in and around Center City, while Latino and Asian populations increased throughout the city. By 2000, Philadelphia was roughly 43 percent white, 43 percent Black, 9 percent Latino, and 5 percent Asian.[1]

The geographic concentration of traditionally upper-income white liberal reformers was reflected in the fact that, of the city's sixty-six wards (divided into 1,692 divisions, distributed among the wards based on population), in 2000 only five were considered "open," meaning that the committee people elected in the divisions voted openly on candidate endorsements and were thus not "machine-controlled" through the Democratic City Committee. The open wards were located in Center City (Fifth and Eighth Wards), Chestnut Hill (Ninth Ward), West Philadelphia (the Twenty-Seventh, which was slightly more diverse but also with a large upper-income white population), and the Graduate Hospital neighborhood southwest of Center City (the Thirtieth, which became open in the 1990s due, in part, to gentrification).[2] (See Figure 3.1.)

In both 1999 and 2003, former council president John Street was elected mayor against Republican nominee Sam Katz, a nominal Republican with close ties to the city's Democrats, but endorsed by the GOP due to his name recognition from running for mayor, in 1991, and governor, in 1994, and a strong fundraising record. Actual Republicans were clearly reluctant to run in a race they assumed they would lose, as registered GOP voters had declined from 235,477 to 192,615 between the 1987 and the 1995 general elections.[3] Yet, Street beat Katz in 1999 by less than 2 percent, or 7,228 votes—a slim victory comparable to Goode's victory over Rizzo in 1987 and Tate's over Specter in 1967.

Similar to the Goode-Rizzo contest, race was a dominant factor in 1999, in which estimates suggest Street (who is Black) captured slightly more than 20 percent of the white vote but close to 94 percent of the Black vote.[4] Unlike Goode but similar to Tate, Street could not credibly campaign as a reform candidate; in the Democratic primary he faced the more reform-oriented Black candidates John White and Dwight Evans, who had both come up through the "Northwest Alliance" of Black politicians led by the late congressman William Gray III. In the general election, the city's white reform voters leaned toward Katz, who won majorities in the Fifth, Eighth, and Ninth Wards, while Street won majorities in the Twenty-Seventh and Thirtieth Wards.

Similar to Tate as well, Street's slim victory in 1999 depended on a tenuous coalition of Black and union voters. Street's union support, especially with respect to the building trades, came from his alliance with electricians' Local 98 business manager John Dougherty. In the 1990s, Dougherty emerged as an independent political force, using his union's funds and its thirty-five hundred members to help elect an increasing number of candidates. As mayor, Street appointed Dougherty chair of the Redevelopment Authority, reappointed him to the airport advisory board, and supported his brother Kevin Dougherty for a city judgeship.[5]

Street's alliance with Dougherty put him in one of two overlapping Democratic factions, the other being led by state senator Vincent Fumo, Demo-

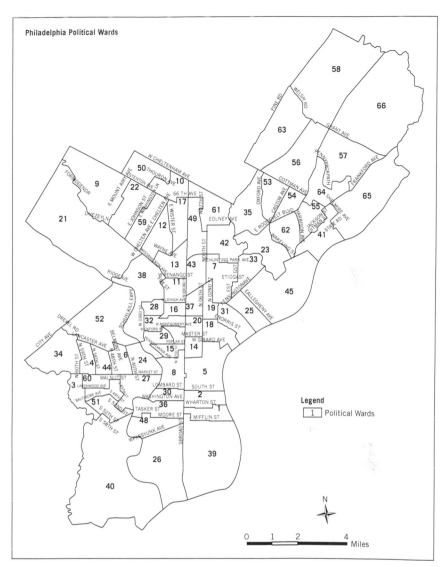

Figure 3.1 Contemporary wards in Philadelphia. The ward boundaries have remained the same since 1965, though division boundaries have changed to accommodate population changes. (See "Genealogy of Philadelphia Political Subdivisions," Department of Records, City of Philadelphia, available at www.phila .gov/phils/docs/inventor/graphics/wards/wards.htm. Accessed April 13, 2020.)

cratic chair of the Pennsylvania Senate Appropriations Committee who, over three decades, had built an extensive network of alliances, allegiances, and patronage that extended into such things as the Philadelphia Board of Education, Delaware River Port Authority, and city council, where Rick Mariano, Frank DiCicco, Jim Kenney, and Anna Verna (council president after Street) were typically identified as "Fumocrats," mostly representing the traditionally blue-collar Rizzocrat wards that stretched from South Philadelphia, along the "river wards" and into the Northeast.

Political factions were loose and fluctuated with specific issues and politicians' ambitions, among other things, even as they were sometimes depicted in the press as parts of a monolithic "machine," with long-standing Democratic City Committee chairman and congressman Bob Brady as the "boss." Yet, much of Brady's job was evidently coordinating among a network of large and small power brokers and upstarts.[6] As long-standing city politician Robert O'Donnell once put it, "The party is neither a monolith nor an organization that's falling apart. The truth is the party is just like a place where people come together."[7]

Street started his mayoralty in 2000 with contentious negotiations over the financing and placement of new sports stadiums and the state government's takeover of the city's schools and patronage-rich parking authority,[8] while also developing and launching his signature Neighborhood Transformation Initiative (NTI), the centerpiece of which was a nearly $300 million bond issue to pay for demolishing fourteen thousand buildings and assembling the cleared land into plots large enough and cleared of tangled titles so as to attract new development.[9]

As the 2003 election came into focus, NTI had made little progress, and the city was battling a rising crime rate.[10] A month before the election, with polls indicating another toss-up race between Street and Katz, a listening device was found in the mayor's office, which the FBI acknowledged was theirs and proceeded to seize documents from a wide array of city officials and people who did extensive contract work for the city, including a chief fundraiser and ally of the mayor and a company who had hired the mayor's brother, Milton Street.[11]

No charges were brought against Mayor Street, but twelve people were indicted and the subsequent trials went into 2005. For the purposes of the 2003 mayoral election, in a strategy for which political consultants Frank Keel and David Axelrod both claim credit, Democrats blamed U.S. attorney general John Ashcroft of attempting to elect a Republican mayor (Katz) to help George W. Bush win Pennsylvania's electoral votes in 2004.[12] With the fresh memory of the 2000 election, in which Democrat Al Gore won the popular vote but the electoral college majority hung on contested election results in

Florida, where Bush's brother was governor, and in which the Supreme Court in a 4–5 partisan decision effectively decided the election for Bush, suspected Republican motivations for the Street investigation, however unfounded, resonated with an increasingly polarized electorate. Katz's support declined precipitously, and Street was reelected in 2003 with 58 percent of the vote.

Yet, the FBI investigations also exposed the prevalence of the "pay to play" system, in which campaign contributions and other payments brought preferential treatment in awarding city contracts. Other highly publicized federal investigations helped reveal a general culture of political corruption, most notably of Fumo, accused of steering illicit payments from various companies into community nonprofits he controlled (he was indicted in 2007 and convicted in 2009), and also of councilman Mariano (a former Fumocrat-turned-Dougherty ally), who before being convicted on bribery charges in 2005 climbed to the top of City Hall Tower in a suspected suicide attempt that drew ample media attention.[13] Simultaneous news reports of council members collecting hundreds of thousands of dollars through a loophole in the city pension plan further stoked public dissatisfaction.[14]

Media coverage of federal investigations was similar to exposés that catalyzed reform movements in the 1900s and 1950s. Yet, the 1905 gas lease revolt was an affair of media and public indignation, not legal action; and revelations of corruption in the 1950s began with a mayoral committee and business reform groups and led to investigations and convictions by city and state—not federal—officials. By contrast, corruption exposés in the 2000s did not originate with the media (in the grips of being transformed by the internet) but with federal agents. There was certainly dissatisfaction over corruption as there had been in the 1900s and 1950s: Polling in 2007 found that majorities of Philadelphians thought "city government was 'pretty much run by a few big interests looking out for themselves,'" "city officials 'waste a lot of money,'" and "'quite a few' officials were corrupt."[15] But there was no public response as there had been in the 1900s and no broad reform coalition as there had been in the 1950s. As one local reporter observed in 2005, "Philadelphians may love to grumble about the lack of integrity in City Hall. . . . But they certainly aren't bombarding Council members with letters or phone calls on the issue."[16]

Philadelphia in the 2000s was less populous, poorer, and more economically and racially divided, with a weaker local press, which, when combined with larger national trends of declining civic participation since the 1970s,[17] made the kinds of reform coalitions from the 1950s and 1960s less likely. The increasing role of federal officials in investigating and prosecuting local corruption was almost an admission that city officials no longer had the capacity or willingness to do so. The Committee of Seventy had been revived in 2005 under the leadership of former *Daily News* editor Zack Stalberg and new board members—"meant to signal a greater commitment by Philadelphia's business community to improving a political culture that has been poisoned by a slew of City Hall–related indictments and convictions"—though it still had no political operation as it had in the early twentieth century.[18] The Pennsylvania Economy League (PEL—renamed the Economy League of Greater Philadelphia in 2007) was no longer a partner to city officials and business reformers, as it had been in the 1930s and 1950s, but a sort-of chamber of commerce that did consulting work. There were hints of reform efforts driven by younger professionals concentrated in Center City, most prominently Young Involved Philadelphia (YIP), formed in 2001. Yet, unlike the reform groups of the earlier twentieth century that had built political organizations, YIP was at least initially more like earlier groups such as the Committee of 100; a social club with a civic purpose, though it would become increasingly active in the gentrifying wards around Center City.

However disingenuous the Democratic political narrative around the 2003 Street scandal had been, it was in part effective because it suggested the reality of a new relationship between national and local politics, catalyzed by Philadelphia's role as the primary source of Democratic votes in a nationally significant swing state. Thus, local activism, especially of the more progressive variety, was increasingly catalyzed by national presidential campaigns. An early case in point was a new set of progressive groups that emerged out of the 2004 presidential campaigns, especially for Howard Dean, that focused more on reform at the ward level—most prominently Philadelphia Neighborhood Networks (PNN). An inaugural PNN meeting in 2005 included some 340 people, representing half the wards in the city, "with the highest concentration of members in traditionally liberal areas," including Center City, Chestnut Hill, "and the 15th Ward in Fairmount. About 25 people came from various West Philadelphia wards."[19] In the 2006 ward elections, PNN and affiliated groups—Philly for Change, YIP, the Young Democrats, and Liberty City Democrats—ran "at least 100 candidates" and won 64 committee seats in various of these wards.[20]

In city council, in direct response to FBI revelations, mayoral aspirant, self-styled reformer, and Northwest Alliance protégé Michael Nutter introduced and got passed a proposed charter amendment creating campaign finance rules limiting "pay for play," which was included as a ballot measure in the 2005 November election. The measure passed overwhelmingly with the active support of "a coalition of civic groups—including Philadelphia Forward, the Pennsylvania Economy League, the Committee of Seventy, and Neighborhood Networks."[21] Many of these same groups became supporters of Nutter in what was initially an underdog mayoral campaign in 2007.

Michael Nutter, Reform, and an Unequal but Resurgent City

As candidates announced their plans, in 2007, to replace Mayor Street, Philadelphia's population increased for the first time in more than fifty years. The schools and hospitals that had accumulated in the city since the eighteenth century were reinvigorated by the "baby boom echo" increase in college-age students and aging baby boomers who needed more medical care. By 2008, education and health services represented 30 percent of all jobs in the city, while hospitality and leisure, and business and professional services, represented another 20 percent. Manufacturing, the backbone of the city's economy for more than a century, represented 4 percent of the city's workforce in 2008, down from 20 percent in 1980.[22]

Service sector job growth provided the basis for a new round of union organizing; the jobs also clustered in and around Center City where many white-collar families thus chose to live, stoking discussions of "gentrification." A 2016 Pew Charitable Trusts report identified 15 of the city's 372 residential census tracts, nearly all adjacent to Center City, as having gentrified from 2000 to 2014. While the citywide population had increased by 2 percent, the white population had decreased by 6 percent and the Black population by 1 percent, and median household incomes had decreased by slightly more than $6,000; in the gentrified tracts, population increased by 13 percent, with the white population increasing 14 percent while the Black population decreased by 18 percent, and household incomes increased by nearly $24,000.[23]

Increased housing demand in gentrifying neighborhoods combined with a ten-year property tax abatement for new and renovated houses, implemented in 2001, drove a construction boom,[24] which, in turn, empowered planning and design advocates, who established two new organizations in 2002, in response to their perceived neglect under Rendell and Street: The Design Advocacy Group, a "salon" formed by members of the defunct Foundation for Architecture, and Penn Praxis, an "applied" organization established as part of the Penn School of Design with Design Advocacy Group cofounder Harris Steinberg appointed its director.[25] In city council, Frank DiCicco and Jim Kenney proposed a charter amendment included on the ballot in the 2007 election, to create a new Zoning Code Commission that would revise the city's outdated zoning code.[26]

Campaign finance, ward-level insurgencies, and planning reform would have all been familiar to reformers in the 1950s and possibly even to those in the 1900s and 1910s. A newer version of reform that defined the 2007 elections was "sustainability"—an idea that emerged from efforts such as the Clinton Climate Initiative that cities were key locations for environmental policies.

As Nutter noted in his memoir, "The sustainability community was probably the most organized group during the 2007 election."[27] In response, every Democratic primary candidate in 2007 issued a "green paper" outlining their sustainability plan.

The sustainability community's ties to reform were reflected in the Next Great City Coalition (NGCC), organized for the 2007 election with a ten-point plan—largely reiterated in Nutter's green paper—for improving the city's environmental performance but also including issues such as zoning. The coalition of sixty-six NGCC "endorsing organizations," included a mix of environmental groups, business groups (most with an environmental focus), unions, members of the old civil rights coalition, several neighborhood civic associations, and reform organizations including the Committee of Seventy, YIP, and PNN (Table 3.1).

TABLE 3.1 ENDORSING ORGANIZATIONS OF THE NEXT GREAT CITY COALITION

- 10,000 Friends of Pennsylvania
- Action Alliance of Senior Citizens of Greater Philadelphia
- AFL-CIO, Philadelphia Council
- AFSCME District Council 47
- AFSCME District Council Local 2187
- American Institute of Architects, Philadelphia Chapter
- American Lung Association of Pennsylvania
- Audubon Pennsylvania
- Bella Vista United Civic Association
- Building Industry Association of Philadelphia
- Chestnut Hill United Methodist Church
- Citizens for Pennsylvania's Future
- Clean Air Council
- Clean Water Action
- Committee of Seventy
- Concerned Block Captains of West and Southwest Philadelphia
- Congreso de Latinos Unidos
- Delaware Valley Green Building Council
- Design Advocacy Group of Philadelphia
- East Falls Tree Tenders
- Francisville Neighborhood Development Corporation
- Free Schuylkill River Park
- Greater Bustleton Civic League Inc.
- Greater Philadelphia Urban Affairs Coalition
- Habitat for Humanity Philadelphia
- Institute for the Study of Civic Values

(continued on next page)

TABLE 3.1 ENDORSING ORGANIZATIONS OF THE NEXT GREAT CITY COALITION (*continued from previous page*)

- Logan Square Neighborhood Association
- NAACP Philadelphia
- Neighborhood Interfaith Movement
- Neighborhoods Now (formerly Philadelphia Neighborhood Development Collaborative)
- Neighbors Allied for the Best Riverfront
- New Kensington Community Development Corporation
- The Partnership CDC
- Passyunk Square Civic Association
- PennEnvironment
- Pennsylvania Environmental Council
- Pennsylvania Horticultural Society
- Pennsylvania Interfaith Climate Change Campaign
- Pennsylvania Parent-Teacher Association
- PenTrans
- Philadelphia Area Project on Occupational Safety and Health (PhilaPOSH)
- Philadelphia Association of Community Development Corporations
- Philadelphia Corporation for Aging
- Philadelphia Neighborhood Networks
- Philadelphia Parks Alliance
- PhillyCarShare
- Philly for Change
- Project NEAT (the Neighborhood Environmental Action Team)
- Queen Village Neighbors Association
- Recycling Alliance of Philadelphia
- Residents of Shawmont Valley Association
- Right to Know Committee
- Roxborough Greenspace Project
- Schuylkill Center for Environmental Education
- Sierra Club Southeastern Pennsylvania Group
- Society Created to Reduce Urban Blight (SCRUB)
- Society for Ecological Restoration
- Society Hill Civic Association
- Sustainable Business Network of Greater Philadelphia
- SustainUS Philadelphia
- University City Green Inc.
- Wallace Roberts and Todd
- Welcoming Center for New Pennsylvanians
- Women's Community Revitalization Project
- Women's Health and Environmental Network
- Young Involved Philadelphia

Source: Karen Black, *Next Great City Philadelphia*, 2007 (Philadelphia: n.p., n.d.)

The NGCC played a role in the 2007 mayoral election similar to that of the Citizens' Charter Committee with respect to charter reform in 1951. A key difference was the transition away from activist business executives and white-collar professionals to professional philanthropists. While the Citizens' Charter Committee had been spearheaded by the business-oriented Greater Philadelphia Movement (GPM), NGCC was funded by the William Penn Foundation, a legacy of chemical magnate Otto Haas, which, in 2010, had approximately $2 billion in assets and distributed nearly $100 million in grants in the Philadelphia region for various efforts, including such reform-oriented projects as a Penn Praxis–led "vision plan" for the Delaware River waterfront that brought together several thousand participants in a public design review process.[28]

The William Penn Foundation and Pew Charitable Trusts (established by the children of Standard Oil founder and arch conservative John Pew) were also key funders driving the evolution of regional media into digital platforms. In 2008, Pew established the Philadelphia Research Initiative and appointed as its director a former *Inquirer* editor, with the intent of providing regular reports on key policy issues.[29] Among other media ventures, the William Penn Foundation provided funding for "The Next Mayor" website, created by the *Daily News* in partnership with the Committee of Seventy and WHYY (the public radio station and National Public Radio affiliate) to provide content regarding the 2007 mayoral campaigns; the planning news website PlanPhilly, established by Penn Praxis in 2006; and Newsworks, founded by WHYY, in 2010, to provide original local news journalism and content from partner websites.[30] Similarly, in 2016, the company that owned the *Inquirer*, *Daily News*, and Philly.com—which had been sold three times between 2006 and 2012, dropping in price from $515 million to $55 million—was donated by its final owner Gerry Lenfest to the Lenfest Institute for Journalism, signaling the city's nearly full transition away from commercial to nonprofit news organizations, except for television.[31]

A novel aspect of the 2007 mayoral race was the absence of Sam Katz, further exposing the weakness of the Philadelphia GOP. By 2008, registered Democrats had reached a near record high of 78.2 percent of voters, and Republicans a record low of 13 percent.[32] The Democratic primary included Nutter, state legislator Dwight Evans, wealthy insurance entrepreneur Tom Knox, and two long-standing members of Congress, Chaka Fattah and Bob Brady—with Brady often suspected of running primarily to take votes away from Knox. In a striking departure from 1999 and 2003, race was a muted feature of the 2007 contest. The Democratic primary included three Black (Fattah, Evans, Nutter) and two white (Brady, Knox) candidates. Polling indicated that, among Black likely voters Fattah had the most support, Knox and Evans were tied for second, but Nutter had the most support among Black people who "described themselves as white-collar professionals."[33] Knox maintained his greater support among likely Black voters, while Nutter's support was concentrated among a recognizable reform coalition of white-collar Black and white people from reform wards.[34]

Nutter won the primary with 37 percent of the vote, winning majorities in nearly every ward in the West, Southwest, Northwest, and Center City; Knox won 25 percent with majorities in wards throughout the Northeast. Primary voters also approved the Zoning Code Commission, whose thirty-three members spent the next four years drafting a new code, approved by the city council at the end of 2011.[35] Nutter beat Republican nominee Al Taubenberger in the general election by 83 percent, but his plurality primary win suggests a muted reform victory like those of the 1880s, 1910s, or 1990s rather than those in the 1950s. Similarly, none of the explicitly "progressive reform" candidates running for at-large council, including PNN cofounder Marc Stier, won a seat.[36]

Nutter's election was the first sign of a new reform cycle. The new mayor was a self-defined reformer and generally recognized as such in the local news. In his first budget, Nutter proposed increased funding for the police, parks, recycling, and the community college; cutting the city's business privilege tax; and establishing a 311 nonemergency call-in system and an Office of Sustainability. Most significantly, from the standpoint of reforms that might have a transformative effect on city politics, and thus qualify as defining a reform cycle, were Nutter's new anticorruption and campaign finance initiatives. He established the position of chief integrity officer (CIO) and—once again reflecting the reform role of federal investigators and prosecutors—hired former prosecutors from the U.S. Attorney's Office for the CIO and city inspector general positions who "had been involved in high-profile anticorruption cases involving the Philadelphia government."[37] Nutter also strengthened the 2005 pay-to-play campaign finance law by interpreting it so that contribution limits applied to not only individual but also "bundled" contributions, thereby making it one of the strongest such laws in the country; as such, it effectively ended most of the large contributions traditionally given by law firms, insurance companies, and developers—but not unions, whose contributions depended on member fees and were later diverted to political action committees (PACs), especially after the U.S. Supreme Court's 2010 ruling that "independent spending" by "outside groups" on behalf of campaigns was protected by the First Amendment.

As the U.S. economy collapsed throughout 2008, the city faced a five-year budget deficit of $1.38 billion,[38] prompting forward some reform-oriented initiatives, including the successful dissolution and reorganization of

the agency responsible for property tax assessments (the notoriously inefficient board of revision of taxes, a patronage hive created in 1854),[39] a proposed "soda tax," and the proposed sale of the city-owned Philadelphia Gas
Works (PGW). The proposed two-cent-per-ounce soda tax was intended to
both balance the municipal budget and address obesity, which in 2006 affected nearly 22 percent of school-age children in the city—a public health
reform similar to those from the early twentieth century, such as Blankenburg's milk inspection program. Trade associations and unions—most notably the Pennsylvania Beverage Association and the Teamsters—quickly mo-
bilized against the proposal, and Nutter never offered a formal bill. In 2011,
Nutter once again proposed the soda tax as a means of addressing a school
district fiscal crisis, but the city council instead approved a property tax increase.[40]

Nutter's comfort in proposing tax increases during an election year suggests what little reelection competition the mayor of a one-party city expected; the 2011 mayoral election was remarkable only for the fact that the
firefighters' union and DC 33, smarting from budget cuts and contract disputes, endorsed Nutter's primary challenger Milton Street, John Street's
brother and a former state senator who had served jail time for failing to file
tax forms.[41] Elsewhere, there were further signs of reform. Among the three
elected officials responsible for administering elections, Stephanie Singer
defeated long-term incumbent Marge Tartaglione for one of two Democratic
seats while Al Schmidt (who would later become famous for his role in the
2020 presidential election) won the single Republican seat, both campaigning on explicit reform pledges.[42] In city council, five older members announced
their retirements and at-large Republican member Frank Rizzo (son of the
former mayor) lost his primary, guaranteeing at least six new members. Yet,
generational turnover did not necessarily translate into reform; four new
district council members (Cindy Bass, Bobby Henon, Kenyatta Johnson, and
Mark Squilla) "owe[d] their elections to established interests, including ward
leaders and unions."[43]

Perhaps, most consequentially, Street protégé Darrell Clarke became the
new council president and, in that role, thwarted Nutter's attempt to sell
PGW, the largest municipally owned gasworks in the country. PGW had
once been at the heart of the city's political machine, but, by 2011, it was the
utility's relative efficiency under effective leadership and low interest rates
that made it a valuable asset, the sale of which might help address the city's
$4.9 billion unfunded pension liability (its assets compared to what it owed
retired city workers). Nutter proposed the PGW sale in 2012 and by the end
of the year had a likely buyer. The sale was supported by the Committee of
Seventy and the Chamber of Commerce while Clarke and a majority of coun-

Figure 3.2 Council president Darrell Clarke standing in front of the council president's chair at the front of city council chambers, 2015. (Taken by Philadelphia City Council, December 10, 2015. Accessed via Wikimedia Commons. Licensed under CC BY 4.0.)

cil members along with city controller Alan Butkovitz publicly doubted it would net the $500 million Nutter claimed it would. City council effectively vetoed the sale in 2014;[44] according to Nutter, "It got ensnared in concerns about who was going to win politically and who was not, and about which person didn't want this or that person to score a big win."[45] (See Figure 3.2.)

Gentrification and Reform

The final years of Nutter's mayoralty were marked by a maturing network of mostly white middle- and upper-middle-class reform groups, defined by at least four characteristics. First, reformers were located primarily in gentrifying wards; building on the efforts of groups such as PNN in the previous decade, they led insurgent campaigns for committee positions in the Second, Thirtieth, and Thirty-Sixth Wards, which stretched from the Schuylkill to the Delaware Rivers immediately south of Center City. These insurgencies were driven in part by generational turnover but also by recruitment and training efforts by groups such as the Philadelphia Chapter of the National Organization for Women, the Coalition of Labor Union Women, YIP, the Bread and Roses Community Fund, and city commissioner Stephanie Singer.[46]

The Thirty-Sixth Ward insurgency highlighted the tensions between gentrification and reform. Ori Feibush, a white developer born and raised in the suburbs who had established a real estate company in the Point Breeze neighborhood in 2008, supported and enlisted more than one hundred new candidates to run for eighty-two committee positions in the ward's 2014 election and paid the legal fees for challenging seventy-six nominating petitions. One analysis found that "the average candidate whose petition was challenged bought their house in 1991 for $18,934. The average person who challenged a petition bought their house in 2010 for $174,944."[47] The latter were the kinds of homes built and sold by Feibush, an outspoken and often intemperate critic who spoke in the reformist language of fixing "broken" city agencies. His efforts at stoking a ward-based insurgency were part of a plan to get him elected in 2015 to the Second District Council seat that included Point Breeze and was held since 2012 by Kenyatta Johnson (who Feibush called a "poverty pimp"), a Black lifetime neighborhood resident and former state representative who had worked as a staffer for state senator Anthony Williams.[48]

A second characteristic of the new reform movement was its focus on planning and land use, with younger activists favoring such things as bike lanes, higher-density housing, less parking, and urbanist amenities such as beer gardens.[49] These issues were, in part, an extension of the politics that had pushed forward the 2007–2011 zoning code reform, which in attempting to regularize land use regulation also came into conflict with "councilmanic prerogative"—the broad right that district council members had in their districts over the sale of city-owned lots and to make exceptions to the zoning code—and which had "played a role in the cases of all six council members convicted of wrongdoing since 1981."[50] Indeed, another prong of Feibush's attack against Johnson was a lawsuit that would later metastasize into an FBI investigation, claiming that Johnson had used councilmanic prerogative to block the sale to Feibush of neighborhood properties.[51]

Third, the newer reform groups in and around Center City used PACs, a legal device used to raise money around specific issues and in support of—but "uncoordinated" with—candidate campaigns. The reform PACs were mostly small but significant in representing the interests of millennial urbanists, such as PhillySetGo and 5th Square. More significant was 3.0 formed in 2014 with money from parking lot magnate Joseph Zuritsky, and other anonymous donors, and led by Alison Perelman (granddaughter of the late philanthropist Raymond Perelman and one of the reform insurgents elected committee person in the Second Ward in 2014) with political director Thomas Hurst who had led an attempted insurgency in the Thirtieth Ward. Reflecting the business orientation of its primary founders, Hurst described 3.0 as falling "between the Greater Philadelphia Chamber of Commerce and the Committee of Seventy" in orientation.[52] Yet, unlike either of those groups, as a PAC, 3.0 was focused both on providing financial support specifically to city council candidates and on "term limits and taxes, pension reform and development projects, school funding and 'low-wage workers.'"[53] The organization counts as its greatest victory its help in electing Jamie Gauthier over twenty-seven-year-incumbent Jannie Blackwell in 2019 to the Third City Council District, which covers virtually all of West Philadelphia and was previously held since 1974 by Blackwell's husband Lucien. Gauthier, a former executive director of the Sustainable Business Network (an NGCC endorsing organization) and the Fairmount Park Conservancy, campaigned against gentrification and Blackwell's use of councilmanic prerogative, among other things.[54]

Fourth, the new reformers were an integral part of the changing media landscape. As former committee person Karen Bojar noted, "Young political writers/reporters such as Patrick Kerkstra, Ryan Briggs, Jon Geeting, Holly Otterbein, and others contributed to the increased interest in the 2014 committeeperson elections."[55] Geeting, for instance, was a cofounder of 5th Square and one of the insurgents elected as committee person in 2014 in the Second Ward (along with Perelman and two former YIP presidents). He became engagement editor for PlanPhilly, in 2015, then director of engagement for 3.0, in 2016, and had earlier "amassed a social media following as the go-to resource for all things Philly urbanism. He cultivated a passionate (and private) Facebook group of planners, city administrators and thought leaders to debate various ideas on how to improve public space in the city."[56] In addition to such outlets as the *Inquirer, Philadelphia Magazine*, and WHYY (where Kerkstra, Otterbein, and Briggs had all worked), a host of new niche-based, reform-oriented, and "solutions"-based websites emerged just at the time of the 2014 ward insurgencies, including the *Philadelphia Citizen*, founded in 2013 by former *Philadelphia Magazine* and *Daily News* editor Larry Platt, and *Billy Penn*, founded in 2014 by the Virginia-based Spirited Media company and acquired by WHYY in 2019.

In 2015, Johnson resoundingly defeated Feibush in the Second District Democratic primary, suggesting Feibush's weakness as a candidate, the limits of gentrification-based reform, and the power of incumbency in district council races. By contrast, there was significant competition in the at-large council races, where the margins of victory were often slim and thus the powers of incumbency weak, and in which twenty-three candidates vied for seven seats. Among the winners were Helen Gym, a former teacher and community activist who had the financial support of the teachers' union; Allan Domb, a realtor known as the "condo king" who sold high-end Center City properties and who in classic reform fashion focused his campaign on bringing his business acumen to city government; and Derek Green, a former aide to retiring Northwest Alliance council member Marian Tasco, who had run for an at-large seat as a reform candidate in 2007 and who was the only one out of four 3.0-backed at-large candidates to win a seat in 2015.[57] (See Figure 3.3.)

Gym and Domb represented what *Philadelphia Citizen* founder Larry Platt described as "Progressives versus Reformers." Reflecting the traditional reformer orientation that he shared with groups such as 3.0, Platt lauded Domb as a pragmatist who sought to "chip away at a long-entrenched insider culture that is driven by Philly's own unique type of machine-driven political ideology," while the progressives, of which Platt declared Gym the leader, were uncompromising class warriors who sought to insert national issues into city politics.[58] However accurate Platt's depiction, it is notable that both Gym and Domb received some of their strongest voter support in the same places, and likely among the same voters, namely those from the traditional Center City reform wards (the Fifth and Eighth) and the neighboring Thirtieth (Graduate Hospital), which also happen to include some of

Figure 3.3 Five of the more recently elected members of Philadelphia City Council. *From left:* Kendra Brooks of the Working Families Party, elected at-large in 2019; Allan Domb, elected at-large in 2015; Jamie Gauthier, elected to the Third District in 2019; Derek Green, elected at-large in 2015; and Cindy Bass, elected to the Eighth District in 2011. (Office of Strategic Marketing and Communications, Temple University, Philadelphia, PA.)

**TABLE 3.2 VOTE PERCENTAGE FOR AT-LARGE CANDIDATES
IN THE TRADITIONAL "OPEN" REFORM WARDS, 2015**

Ward	5	8	9	27	30
Helen Gym	**17**	17	**18**	**19**	**17**
Alan Domb	16	**17**	14	14	16
Derek Green	14	14	15	16	15
William Greenlee	13	13	14	15	14
Blondell Reynolds Brown	12	12	14	16	15

Source: Jonathan Tannen, "Ward Data Portal," Sixty Six Wards blog, available at sixtysixwards.com.
Accessed April 13, 2020.
Note: The candidates listed are those Democrats who won in this election, in which voters get to vote for five
candidates and the top five vote-getters win at-large seats. Two additional seats are reserved for the top vote-
getters among the minority parties. In each ward, the percentage win of the candidate who won the most
votes is in bold.

the highest-income neighborhoods in the city (Table 3.2).[59] Judging by their
electoral support both Gym and Domb could claim the mantle of reformer
in the traditional sense—Gym possibly more so in the sense that she advo-
cated for a new vision of the city that was more equitable and inclusive, and
which overlapped significantly, at least in the abstract, with the priorities of
groups such as 3.0.

Mayor Jim Kenney and President Donald Trump

Polling indicated three viable candidates in the 2015 Democratic mayoral
primary: Former DA Lynne Abraham, council member Jim Kenney, and
state senator Anthony Williams. By the end of April, Kenney pulled ahead
as he racked up endorsements from the AFL-CIO, DC 33, several prominent
Black and Latino officials, LGBT leaders, and the police, teachers', electricians', firefighters', and hospital and health care workers' unions. He enjoyed
a broad fundraising base, particularly through union and LGBT group PACs
who spent more than $4 million in support of his campaign. Williams got
more PAC support but almost all of it came from the founders of a suburban
financial firm, and almost exclusively because of Williams's support of charter schools. With little PAC support, Abraham trailed in advertising and
other forms of outreach. Kenney, ultimately, won the primary by 56 percent,
a unique accomplishment considering that the last Democratic nonincum-
bent mayoral candidate to win a primary with a majority of votes was Wilson Goode in 1983. He then won the general election by 85 percent against
a largely unknown Republican challenger.[60]

Kenney's electoral coalition included not just progressives and reformers but also what remained of more conservative blue-collar white voters.

He was, after all, a traditional South Philadelphia Fumocrat who had long served as Fumo's district chief of staff. Speaking of his first victory when he ran for at-large council, in 1991, he noted: "It had nothing to do with me. It was all the political deals, getting the money and, without a doubt, the support and help of Vince Fumo and Bob Brady."[61] Kenney was wonkish and outspoken but relatively conservative; described in the *Inquirer* during his second council term, in 1997, as "a distinctive, populist and often-contrarian voice in Philadelphia politics, an outspoken critic of the public schools, of civilian oversight of the Police Department, and of most of the liberal agenda put forth by his colleagues on Council."[62]

Yet, as an at-large council member, Kenney faced competitive elections, compelling him to expand beyond his Fumocrat base. For instance, by the 1980s, fueled by AIDS activism, gay rights advocates had become a significant political force, and, thus, by the mid-1990s, Kenney had become one of their key council allies and, in the 2010s, was the chief sponsor of LGBT equality and hate crime legislation (it is worth noting that Fumo had also been a long-standing gay rights advocate).[63] And, as the sustainability community played an evidently outsize role in the 2007 elections, Kenney played a lead role in establishing a new council committee on the environment and served as its first chair.

In 2015, Kenney campaigned on a progressive agenda similar to the successful 2013 campaigns of Bill de Blasio in New York, Ed Murray in Seattle, and Betsy Hodges in Minneapolis. Some of Kenney's chief campaign pledges were to establish universal prekindergarten, expand the Philadelphia port, end "stop and frisk" police practices, decriminalize marijuana, and support new immigrants. On these and other issues, he had a long-standing record and was able to run left of Williams and Abraham. Williams appeared beholden to charter school interests while Abraham was best known for her aggressive pursuit of the death penalty and life sentences as DA in the 1990s and 2000s—punishments that fell disproportionately on the city's Black population. By contrast, as one pollster put it, Kenney's position on marijuana decriminalization communicated "that he understood the impact of harsh drug laws and unequal enforcement in minority communities."[64]

Kenney's mayoral agenda began with universal prekindergarten, which he planned to fund with the soda tax—a fact that, though he had twice failed to support the soda tax when Nutter was mayor, indicated that Kenney was following in the same reform cycle as had Nutter. Despite fierce opposition from the Teamsters and the beverage industry, the city council approved a 1.5 cent-per-ounce soda tax.[65]

As the city began implementing the soda tax, FBI agents raided the offices of electricians' Local 98 and council member and Dougherty ally Bobby Henon,[66] and Donald Trump was elected president. The general reaction to Trump's election in liberal Philadelphia—akin to that following a major domestic terrorist attack—combined with the groups that had been organized and energized as part of Bernie Sanders's presidential campaign, created a progressive groundswell that threatened to undo Kenney's diverse electoral coalition. As an example of what could happen, in 2017, Mayor Hodges in Minneapolis lost her reelection bid as she was outflanked on her left by several candidates, including the winner, Jacob Frey. Kenney, who did not face reelection until 2019 (he won easily) looked comparatively progressive, in large part because of his well-publicized fight over Philadelphia's "sanctuary city" status, referring to the city's limited cooperation with federal immigration enforcement, which began as Mayor Nutter's response against the Obama administration's deportation policies. In August 2017, the City of Philadelphia sued the U.S. Department of Justice for putting new conditions on federal funding that would have required the city to share information about immigrants with federal officials, per a Trump executive order.[67] In June 2018, a federal court ruled in favor of Philadelphia and Kenney did a widely publicized "happy dance," which the White House called "disgusting."[68]

The New Progressive Movement and the Future of Philadelphia Politics

The liberal political activism energized by Trump's election was reflected in vastly increased interest in "running for office" workshops organized by 3.0, the Committee of Seventy, PNN—and a new more progressive group, Reclaim, founded by "former staffers and volunteers" from Sanders's presidential campaign.[69] With a liberal-union coalition similar to that of Americans for Democratic Action in the 1950s, Reclaim and other progressive groups (such as 215 People's Alliance and the stalwart PNN) combined with service workers' unions (such as those representing hospital, hotel, and restaurant workers) along with $1.6 million from a PAC affiliated with billionaire George Soros (who was donating to liberal campaigns in cities across the country) to get Larry Krasner elected DA in 2017—arguably the most liberal DA in the city's history, who campaigned on never pursuing the death penalty, ending cash bail, and seeking alternatives to incarceration.[70]

The other electoral upset in 2017 was the city controller election in which Rebecca Rhynhart, a former investment banker who served as city treasurer and budget director under Nutter and as chief administrative officer under Kenney, defeated three-term incumbent Alan Butkovitz by a nearly 20 percent margin. City party leaders interpreted the victories of both Rhynhart and Krasner as part of a generational change among voters, combined with increased activism, reflected in voter turnout that was 50 percent higher than citywide elections in 2009 and 2013.[71] Just like Domb and Gym, Krasner and Rhynhart fell into distinct progressive and reformer categories, respectively; Rhynhart got more support in the more conservative reform wards of Center City while Krasner did better in the more liberal outlying wards, most notably in West Philadelphia.

Krasner's election suggests a new progressive movement, distinct from the more conservative reform movement that fueled Nutter's 2007 election. In one telling contrast, among the sixty groups that joined the progressive coalition Alliance for a Just Philadelphia in 2018 (Table 3.3), and the sixty-six groups that had signed on to the NGCC in 2007, only PNN is on both lists. By 2017, the progressive coalition scored significant victories in the gentrifying First and Second Wards immediately southeast of Center City. In 2018, Reclaim cofounder Nikil Saval won against both Fumocrats and traditional reformers represented by 3.0 to get elected leader of the Second Ward; Reclaim member Adams Rackes was elected leader of the First Ward; and Rackes's wife and former WHYY reporter Elizabeth Fiedler was elected to the Pennsylvania representative seat covering the First Ward. In 2020, Saval was elected to the state senate seat previously held by Fumo and Fumo protégé Larry Farnese (which covers all of Center City and nearly all of South Philadelphia and stretches into the gentrifying neighborhoods of Northern Liberties and Fishtown), and, in West Philadelphia's Twenty-Seventh Ward, Reclaim member Rick Krajewski beat thirty-five-year incumbent James Roebuck for a state representative seat. Reclaim's growing clout was possibly best captured by the fact that electricians' Local 98 donated $50,000 to Saval's senate campaign (though the donation was in part for a grudge held by Dougherty, who had run for the same seat and lost to Farnese).[72] (See Figure 3.4.)

While Reclaim worked within the Democratic Party, it was allied with the WFP, in large part a vehicle for service workers' unions. Founded in New York in 1998, the WFP's first foray into Philadelphia politics was leading a successful movement in 2014 for a city charter amendment requiring subcontractors on city contracts to pay a "living wage" to their workers, supported by largely the same unions that supported Krasner.[73] As a third party, WFP benefited from the erosion of the city's Republicans, who, in 2017, for the first time probably since before the Civil War, were outnumbered by voters registered as independents or for third parties. This was especially significant for the two at-large council seats reserved for a minority party that had been held by Republicans since 1952. In 2019, WFP nominee and community organizer Kendra Brooks (pictured in Figure 3.3)—whose platform emphasized "plans to improve access to affordable housing, ending the

TABLE 3.3 JUSTICE ALLIANCE MEMBER GROUPS

- 215 People's Alliance
- 350 Philadelphia
- ACT UP
- ADAPT
- Almanac Dance Circus Theatre
- Amistad Law Center
- Applied Mechanics
- Asian Americans United
- Be the Change Philadelphia
- Black and Brown Coalition of PHL
- Black and Brown Workers Cooperative
- Black Lives Matter Philly
- Caucus of Working Educators
- The Center for Carceral Communities
- Coalition to End Death by Incarceration
- Disabled in Action
- Earth Quaker Action Team
- Faculty and Staff Federation of CCP
- HIAS Pennsylvania
- Human Rights Coalition
- idiosynCrazy Productions
- IfNotNow Philadelphia
- Indivisible Philadelphia
- in.site collaborative
- Juntos
- Movement Alliance Project
- Mutual Aid Philly
- Neighbors against the Gas Plants
- New Sanctuary Movement of Philadelphia
- Northwest Philadelphia Climate Action Network
- One Pennsylvania
- PA Domestic Workers Alliance
- PA Working Families Organization
- Pennsylvania Debt Collective
- Pennsylvania Immigration and Citizenship Coalition
- Philadelphia Area Cooperative Alliance
- Philadelphia Assembled
- Philadelphia Climate Works
- Philadelphia Community Bail Fund
- Philadelphia Drivers' Union

(continued on next page)

TABLE 3.3 JUSTICE ALLIANCE MEMBER GROUPS
(*continued from previous page*)

- Philadelphia Ethical Society
- Philadelphia Neighborhood Networks
- Philly Childcare Collective
- Philly Power Research Collective
- Philly Schools Unifying Neighborhoods
- Philly Student Union
- Philly Thrive
- Philly Transit Riders Union
- Project Safe
- Reclaim Philadelphia
- Red Umbrella Alliance
- Soil Generation
- Spiral Q
- Stadium Stompers
- Sunrise Philadelphia
- Tikkun Olam Chavurah
- TUFF Girls
- Up against the Law Legal Collective
- Vietlead
- Women's Medical Fund

Source: Alliance for a Just Philadelphia, available at https://ajustphiladelphia.org/#thealliance. Accessed June 12, 2022.

10-year tax abatement, beefing up enforcement of pro-worker ordinances, and implementing a 'Philadelphia Green New Deal' to tackle climate change"[74]—overtook Republican incumbent and former mayoral candidate Al Taubenberger to win a minority seat.

Brooks's victory was a blow not just to the GOP (it prompted the resignation of city committee chair Michael Meehan, replaced by Martina White, a thirty-year-old state representative from the Northeast) but also to the building trades' unions, especially Dougherty's Local 98. Service workers' unions, for whom Brooks served as a proxy, had the advantage of some thirty-six thousand members who lived in the city, in contrast to the building trades' members who lived mostly in the suburbs and thus could not vote.[75] In another blow, also in 2019, federal prosecutors revealed a 116-count indictment against Dougherty, Henon, and six other individuals, including "staggering claims of corruption and political vindictiveness"—Dougherty had, for instance, instructed Henon to hold up the city's cable lease agreement with

Figure 3.4 Nikil Saval (*left*) and Rick Krajewski (*right*) of Reclaim Philadelphia. In 2020, Saval was elected to the Pennsylvania Senate, and Krajewski was elected to the Pennsylvania House of Representatives. (Reclaim Philadelphia.)

Comcast in order to steer $2 million to a favored electrical contractor and to use the city's building code to prevent nonunionized workers from installing MRI machines at Children's Hospital of Philadelphia. In November 2021, both Dougherty and Henon were convicted on multiple counts, and Henon resigned from city council in January 2022.[76]

There were, as well, indications of a rising progressive movement beyond elections, reflecting a shift in the "Overton window" (that is, the range of broadly acceptable policies) affecting reformers and progressives alike and indicating a full-fledged reform cycle, which had begun under Nutter and had veered leftward, especially after 2016. In 2017, the Lenfest Institute funded a "solutions journalism" project around prison reentry that brought together fourteen local news organizations, including the *Citizen*, *Billy Penn*, WHYY, the *Tribune*, and the *Inquirer*. That project has since grown into the solutions-based Resolve Philly media network, covering other topics such as poverty. In 2018, the Economy League of Greater Philadelphia appointed as its executive director Jeff Hornstein, a former organizer for the Service Employees International Union, who focused not on government efficiency and corruption but on "anchor procurement," a redistributive import substitution strategy of supporting local businesses, aimed at the city's educational and medical institutions.

The Future of Philadelphia Politics

When COVID-19 struck Philadelphia in March 2020, Kenney issued a stay-at-home order; nonessential businesses closed, and city unemployment rose from 7 percent to more than 16 percent in one month.[77] The school district closed its 326 schools, sending home more than two hundred thousand children, shootings and murders spiked, and, at the end of May, protests inspired by the killing of George Floyd in Minneapolis sparked riots, looting, demonstrations, and aggressive use of force by the police that compelled the city's managing director to resign. The twenty-four-year incumbent head of DC 33 was voted out of office by municipal workers who felt they did not get enough hazard pay or protective gear. In the public libraries, the newly formed Concerned Black Workers of the Free Library pushed out library director Siobhan Reardon over what they claimed was a "culture of racial discrimination."[78]

The spike in violent crime, which has continued into 2022, might have led to a law-and-order backlash like that which elected Rizzo in 1971, but, in 2021, Larry Krasner once again won the Democratic primary for DA against the best efforts of the Philadelphia Fraternal Order of Police, the largest single donor to Krasner's challenger Carlos Vega, who captured only 33 percent of the vote. And, as a broad array of city politicians have noted, the issue of racial injustice has permeated virtually every policy discussion—according to council member Allan Domb, "Every hearing in the last year—from sheriff sales to vaccine distribution—has included a focus on systemic racism."[79] The rhetoric has been combined with new redistributive policies, such as Darrell Clarke's Neighborhood Preservation Initiative (NPI)—an obvious homage to Street's NTI—an "ambitious antipoverty and affordable-housing plan" funded by a new construction tax and reductions to the tax abatement on new housing construction; a plan opposed by building trades' unions and developers but supported by the Chamber of Commerce, among others.[80]

The varied support for NPI suggests the blurred boundaries between progressives and more conservative reformers, who are divided perhaps less on substance than style, rhetoric, and where they find their financial and electoral support. And, despite progressives' recent victories, more conservative business-oriented reformers have been actively planning. Rhynhart won the 2021 Democratic primary for controller and may well run for mayor in 2023—as might Helen Gym. Outside of elections, a group of civic and business leaders—Drexel president John Fry, Children's Hospital CEO Madeline Bell, venture capitalist Josh Kopelman, bankers Michael Forman and Michael Gerber from FS Investments, and Ryan Boyer from the Laborers' International Union of North America—started meeting in the summer of 2020 to map out the city's post-COVID-19 recovery. Much like the Committee of Seven from 1904 that spawned the Committee of Seventy, this more recent group has spawned a "Saturday Morning Group," a broader but informal gathering of leaders, as well as a more formal nonprofit, the Philadelphia Equity Alliance, housed at the Philadelphia Foundation and led by Keith Bethel, a retired Aramark executive who also serves on the boards of the Urban League and Chamber of Commerce.

Combined, the efforts of progressives and reformers, from Nutter's election in 2007 to at least Reclaim's 2020 electoral victories, constitute a new reform cycle in which insurgents have won elections against an older guard and have focused on potentially transformative policies aimed both at making the city more livable and sustainable and in promoting economic growth for the sake of lifting up its poorest residents, as reflected in NPI. Yet, NPI also reflects a city with both so much wealth and so much poverty that the wealthy can afford redistributive taxes, living in exclusive neighborhoods insulated from poverty and crime, and tolerating corruption. As was true a century earlier, some small number get engaged in reform efforts and enjoy some successes. It is notable that the electoral support of a progressive politician such as Gym comes from wealthier wards where voters ostensibly prefer her policy positions even if they will not benefit from them personally. In the absence of a middle class, redistributive policies can become noblesse oblige—reflected as well in the increasingly prominent policy-making role of philanthropic foundations—and the kind of broad reform coalition that might truly transform the city becomes unlikely if not impossible.

Further reinforcing the fragmentary impulses of economic inequality are the self-reinforcing processes of a weakened and fragmentary press and low voter turnout. Philadelphia news media's transition to nonprofit and foundation ownership has provided some greater stability and the move to niche-based platforms provides some greater diversity of perspectives, but the overall decline in revenues and thus capacity has also led to less investigatory reporting and thus less capacity to participate in and stoke reform efforts. And changes to media are at least partially responsible for declining rates of civic participation, including voting.[81] Looking at mayoral election years between 1951 and 1991, the lowest voter turnout was 60 percent in 1979. By contrast, despite increases from the preceding cycles, turnout in 2017 for the controller and DA races was 20 percent, and, in 2019, for mayor and city council it was 28 percent.[82]

Decreasing turnout in local elections, a national trend, has traditionally benefited machine politicians, especially in Philadelphia for wards positions, state legislative seats, row offices, council districts, and judgeships. Yet, as Reclaim and other groups have proven, low turnout can also be used to the advantage of reformers, especially in ward elections that serve as the bases for winning higher offices. And, in competitive citywide elections, such as for mayor, controller, DA, and at-large council, low turnout can also serve to make the vote of activist reformers more powerful. In short, both the Democratic machine and the reform coalition benefit from low turnout even as it creates a more politically fragmented and less engaged city that is less capable of building public support for more wide-ranging reforms.

These various trend lines can be contrasted to a city that has also become more populous and economically vibrant over the past decade and is thus slowly reinventing itself after a half century of decline—though, whether this growth can be sustained, especially in the wake of COVID-19, remains to be seen. If it can be, it may hold out the promise of a more racially and ethnically diverse city with both a local news media made more vibrant specifically because it is more diverse and fragmented and a new generation of political activists committed to a new vision of Philadelphia as a site of sustainable and equitable urbanism, innovating new ways to address its deeply rooted problems of racial and economic inequality, among others.

CONCLUSION

Philadelphia Politics and
the Passage of Time

The belief in progress—in an infinite perfectibility
understood as an infinite ethical task—and the
representation of eternal return are complementary. They are
the indissoluble antinomies in the face of which the
dialectical conception of historical time must be developed.
In this conception, the idea of eternal return appears
precisely as that "shallow rationalism" which the belief in
progress is accused of being, while faith in progress seems no
less to belong to the mythic mode of thought than does the
idea of eternal return.
—WALTER BENJAMIN, *Arcades Project*, 119.[1]

I have argued that Philadelphia's political history can be described in terms
of cycles, or series of events that resemble and can be usefully compared
to past and future series of events. Such pattern recognition is necessary
to historiography. In the absence of recognizable and repetitive patterns
across time, history becomes an exercise in describing entirely unique past
events that have no contemporary relevance. On the other hand, perfectly
repetitive patterns imply a steady state in which time does not perceptibly
move forward and history does not exist.

Institutions mediate between the extremes of perfect repetitions and the
patternless passage of time. A case in point relevant to the story of Philadelphia reform is elections, which have occurred with such regularity and in-
duce such predictable behaviors that one is practically indistinguishable from
the next, thereby collapsing and potentially eliminating any sense of the passage of time. Yet, elections also structure change, for instance, by providing
opportunities for electing people who in various ways might disrupt the status quo. My argument regarding reform cycles hinges, in part, on such "critical elections" that move time forward by creating a perceptible change, even
as the electoral system itself creates repetitions that slow time down.

All of the various institutions in Philadelphia—the city government, party ward system, universities, businesses, and civic associations, among others—are interconnected but discrete rule systems that structure time in different ways; yet, by virtue of their interconnectedness, change in one institution inevitably results in changes in other institutions. Another relevant case in point is the relationship between party and electoral systems. Parties adapt themselves to the electoral system to win elections and gain control of government, and then they often seek to alter electoral systems to maintain control. At the same time, parties are not monoliths but rather venues for negotiation and debate, the results of which can have unintended consequences that alter the electoral system and thus also affect the parties. Philadelphia's 1919 charter, for instance, was partially a consequence of factional feuds among Organization Republicans, one result of which was that the wards were subsumed into larger council electoral districts, thereby altering both the significance of the wards in elections and, thus, the nature of parties themselves over the long term.

The reform cycles that I have identified in this book were incubated in social networks fostered in various niches scattered throughout Philadelphia's institutional landscape, typically found among business associations, among intellectual communities at universities, in local media outlets, in liberal labor unions, and, more recently, in philanthropic foundations. When these networks were able to extend into the political parties, especially through the wards, they had the ability to alter the larger institutional landscape in complex and unintended ways. The same was true in other cities whose institutional landscapes shared similar features, such as universities, unions, and chambers of commerce, though small changes over time could lead to notably different political trajectories. Though there is hardly space here to compare Philadelphia to other cities in this regard, it is worth noting that simple differences, such as the lack of mayoral term limits, or coterminous ward and council districts, in Chicago, arguably created a different relationship between the city government, elections, and political parties, contributing to the notable lack of a postwar reform movement such as there was in Philadelphia, creating a notably different racial political dynamic in either city (as I noted in Chapter 2), which then contributed to the further difference of Chicago moving to nonpartisan elections.

The reform cycles I have identified are one type of change that alters the institutional construction of time. The role of reform has always been to change how the city functions and what it does in ways meant to signify progress, counterpoised against a machine intent on defending the status quo. The reformers and machine politicians I have discussed were (and are) concerned with practical affairs and would not have much patience for the issues mentioned by Walter Benjamin in my epigram above—that is, whether they pursued progress as part of an "infinite ethical task" or were caught up in some sort of Nietzschean eternal return. Yet, they were very much embroiled in both processes. Reformers have almost always been inspired by images of a new city that they did, in fact, see as more perfect than what currently existed, captured most obviously by Ed Bacon's 1947 Better Philadelphia Exhibition but also by Darrell Clarke's current NPI. And the continuity of reform groups, which have formed a virtually unbroken chain from the 1840s to today, certainly speaks to at least a collectively conceived infinite ethical task, even if any given individual reformer did not necessarily believe in such a thing.

At the other end of the antinomy, it is similarly doubtful that any of Philadelphia's regular organization politicians, from the "hunker" Whigs who opposed municipal railroad subscriptions in the 1840s to the Fumocrat and Dougherty Democrats of the twenty-first century, conceived of themselves as being caught up in an eternal return. Yet, they typically sought to maintain a status quo from which they benefited, and, in that sense, they sought to make time stand still. Older politicians might be replaced by newer ones in elections, but, if the elections occur with perfect regularity and elected officials' jobs are simply to maintain existing policies—if they were, as the *Inquirer* called them in the 1930s, "drones"—it would be hard to argue that time has meaningfully passed or that the elections were not, in fact, an instantiation of an eternal return.

Following Benjamin's logic that both the eternal return and the idea of progress as an infinite ethical task can be defined as mythic modes of thought, the myth in the case of Philadelphia reform cycles is a city—that 130-square-mile territory defined by arbitrary boundaries drawn in the seventeenth century and governed by a system that has evolved in fits and starts over the past 340 years—that is, in some sense, inherently corrupt, virtually always on the brink of some form of collapse, yet also perennially worthy of redemption. However illusory it may be, this myth of Philadelphia is the conceptual glue that has maintained a sense of political identity for more than three centuries.

NOTES

INTRODUCTION

1. A decent summary and discussion of the urban-politics literature through the 1970s can be found in Paul Peterson, *City Limits* (Chicago: University of Chicago Press, 1981).

2. Clarence Stone, *Regime Politics: Governing Atlanta, 1946–1988* (Lawrence: University Press of Kansas, 1989); John Logan and Harvey Molotch, *Urban Fortunes: Toward a Political Economy of Place* (Berkeley: University of California Press, 1987).

3. Jessica Trounstine, *Segregation by Design: Local Politics and Inequality in American Cities* (New York: Cambridge University Press, 2018); Sarah Anzia, "Party and Ideology in American Local Government: An Appraisal," *Annual Review of Political Science* 24 (2021): 133–150.

4. David Mayhew, *Electoral Realignments: A Critique of an American Genre* (New Haven, CT: Yale University Press, 2004).

5. James L. Sundquist, *Dynamics of the Party System: Alignment and Realignment of Political Parties in the United States*, rev. ed. (Washington, DC: Brookings Institution Press, 1983), 253–255.

6. John Kingdon, *Agendas, Alternatives, and Public Policies* (New York: Harper Collins, 1984).

7. Frank Baumgartner and Bryan Jones, *Agendas and Instability in American Politics*, 2nd ed. (Chicago: University of Chicago Press, 2009), chap. 1.

8. The classic account is provided in Buzz Bissinger, *A Prayer for the City* (New York: Random House, 1997).

CHAPTER 1

1. Carl Bridenbaugh, *Cities in the Wilderness: The First Century of Urban Life in America, 1625–1742* (New York: Alfred A. Knopf, 1960), 6, 143, 303; E. Digby Baltzell, *Puritan Boston and Quaker Philadelphia* (Boston: Beacon, 1979), 150.

2. Baltzell, *Puritan Boston and Quaker Philadelphia*, 151–153.

3. Baltzell, *Puritan Boston and Quaker Philadelphia*, 126–132.

4. Baltzell, *Puritan Boston and Quaker Philadelphia*, 118–119, quote on 131; Frederick B. Tolles, *Meeting House and Counting House: The Quaker Merchants of Colonial Philadelphia 1682–1763* (New York: W. W. Norton, 1948), 42–43, chap. 3.

5. Robert E. Wright, *The First Wall Street: Chestnut Street, Philadelphia, and the Birth of American Finance* (Chicago: University of Chicago Press, 2005), 16–27.

6. Domenic Vitiello and George Thomas, *The Philadelphia Stock Exchange and the City It Made* (Philadelphia: University of Pennsylvania Press, 2010), 15.

7. Vitiello and Thomas, *Philadelphia Stock Exchange*, 33.

8. Billy Smith, *The "Lower Sort": Philadelphia's Laboring People, 1750–1800* (Ithaca, NY: Cornell University Press, 1990), 163.

9. Jon Teaford, *The Municipal Revolution in America: Origins of Modern Urban Government, 1650–1825* (Chicago: University of Chicago Press, 1975), 56.

10. Tolles, *Meeting House and Counting House*, 119.

11. Edward Allinson and Boies Penrose, *Philadelphia 1681–1887: A History of Municipal Development* (Philadelphia: Allen, Lane, and Scott, 1887), xlvii–lii.

12. Teaford, *Municipal Revolution*, 57–58.

13. Smith, *The "Lower Sort,"* 165.

14. Teaford, *Municipal Revolution*, 52–62, 82–85.

15. Diane Lindstrom, *Economic Development in the Philadelphia Region, 1810–1850* (New York: Columbia University Press, 1978), 53, 56, 157.

16. Richardson Dilworth, "Drexel, Philadelphia, and the Urban Ecology of Higher Education," in *Building Drexel: The University and Its City, 1891–2016*, ed. Richardson Dilworth and Scott Knowles (Philadelphia: Temple University Press, 2017), 10–11.

17. Philip Scranton, *Proprietary Capitalism: The Textile Manufacture at Philadelphia, 1800–1885* (New York: Cambridge University Press, 1984).

18. Arthur S. Guarino, "Philadelphia Board of Trade," in *Encyclopedia of Greater Philadelphia*, ed. Charlene Mires, Howard Gillette, Randall Miller, and Tamara Gaskell (Camden, NJ: Rutgers University, 2013), available at philadelphiaencyclopedia.org. Accessed June 12, 2022.

19. Sam Bass Warner Jr., *Private City: Philadelphia in Three Periods of Its Growth* (Philadelphia: University of Pennsylvania Press, 1968), 61.

20. Warner, *Private City*, 73.

21. Peter McCaffery, *When Bosses Ruled Philadelphia: The Emergence of the Republican Machine, 1867–1933* (University Park: Pennsylvania State University Press, 1993), 5.

22. Wright, *First Wall Street*, 123.

23. Warner, *Private City*, chap. 7.

24. Andrew Heath, "'The Manifest Destiny of Philadelphia': Imperialism, Republicanism, and the Remaking of a City and Its People, 1837–1877" (Ph.D. diss., University of Pennsylvania, 2008), 128–132. See also Andrew Heath, *In Union There Is Strength: Phila-*

delphia in the Age of Urban Consolidation (Philadelphia: University of Pennsylvania Press, 2019), 43–46.

25. Albert Churella, *The Pennsylvania Railroad*, vol. 1, *Building an Empire, 1846–1917* (Philadelphia, University of Pennsylvania Press, 2013), chap. 3, quote on 89.

26. The $1.5 million figure is from Churella, *Pennsylvania Railroad*, 96–97, though Heath notes that over several years "the municipal investment grew to $5 million" (*In Union There Is Strength*, 82).

27. Churella, *Pennsylvania Railroad*, 100.

28. Andrew Heath, "Consolidation Act of 1854," in *Encyclopedia of Greater Philadelphia*, ed. Charlene Mires, Howard Gillette, Randall Miller, and Tamara Gaskell (Camden, NJ: Rutgers University, 2013), available at philadelphiaencyclopedia.org. Accessed June 12, 2022.

29. Allinson and Penrose, *Philadelphia*, 142–143, 156–228. See also J. Thomas Scharf and Thompson Westcott, *History of Philadelphia, 1609–1884*, vol. 1 (Philadelphia: L. H. Everts, 1884), 713–716.

30. Allinson and Penrose, *Philadelphia*, 142–143, 156–228.

31. Allinson and Penrose, *Philadelphia*, 165–166, quote on 269.

32. Scharf and Westcott, *History of Philadelphia*, vol. 1, 715.

33. Maxwell Whiteman, *Gentlemen in Crisis: The First Century of the Union League of Philadelphia, 1862–1962* (Philadelphia: Union League, 1975), 15–20.

34. McCaffery, *When Bosses Ruled Philadelphia*, 9.

35. McCaffery, *When Bosses Ruled Philadelphia*, 17–22.

36. McCaffery, *When Bosses Ruled Philadelphia*, 22–27.

37. McCaffery, *When Bosses Ruled Philadelphia*, 22–27.

38. McCaffery, *When Bosses Ruled Philadelphia*, 49–51.

39. See Baltzell, *Puritan Boston and Quaker Philadelphia*, 381; Philip S. Benjamin, "Gentlemen Reformers in the Quaker City, 1870–1912," *Political Science Quarterly* 85 (March 1970): 61–79.

40. Domenic Vitiello, *Engineering Philadelphia: The Sellers Family and the Industrial Metropolis* (Ithaca, NY: Cornell University Press, 2013), 107.

41. McCaffery, *When Bosses Ruled Philadelphia*, 51.

42. McCaffery, *When Bosses Ruled Philadelphia*, 53–56.

43. McCaffery, *When Bosses Ruled Philadelphia*, 53–59; James Bryce, *American Commonwealth* (Chicago: Charles H. Sergel, 1891), vol. 2, 377–378.

44. Lucretia Blankenburg, *The Blankenburgs of Philadelphia* (Philadelphia: John C. Winston, 1929), xxvi.

45. McCaffery, *When Bosses Ruled Philadelphia*, 71.

46. Jerome Hodos, "The 1876 Centennial in Philadelphia: Elite Networks and Political Culture," in *Social Capital in the City: Community and Civic Life in Philadelphia*, ed. Richardson Dilworth (Philadelphia: Temple University Press, 2006), 32.

47. Whiteman, *Gentlemen in Crisis*, 131.

48. McCaffery, *When Bosses Ruled Philadelphia*, 54.

49. Allinson and Penrose, *Philadelphia*, 272–276.

50. Clinton Rogers Woodruff, A. Prescott Folwell, John MacVicar, Mrs. William E. D. Scott, Frederick S. Hall, Edmund Billings, Solomon Blum, F. E. Stevens, Max B. May, James J. McLoughlin, John A. Butler, Sydney A. Thomas, Henry L. McCune, J. Allen Smith, and W. G. Joerns, "Notes on Municipal Government. The Activities of Civic

Organizations for Municipal Improvement in the United States: A Symposium," *Annals of the American Academy of Political and Social Science* 25 (March 1905): 180. See also McCaffery, *When Bosses Ruled Philadelphia*, 111.

51. McCaffery, *When Bosses Ruled Philadelphia*, 79–80.

52. William S. Vare, *My Forty Years in Politics* (Philadelphia: Roland Swain, 1933), 46.

53. Vare, *My Forty Years in Politics*, 49.

54. Vare, *My Forty Years in Politics*, 46–47; quote on 47. On Penrose, see John Lukacs, *Philadelphia: Patricians and Philistines, 1900–1950* (New York: Farrar, Straus and Giroux, 1980), chap. 2.

55. Vare, *My Forty Years in Politics*, 79.

56. McCaffery, *When Bosses Ruled Philadelphia*, 86–87, 151–153.

57. Summary information for the Herbert Welsh Collection, Historical Society of Pennsylvania, available at http://www2.hsp.org/collections/manuscripts/w/Welsh0702 .html. Accessed June 12, 2022; George Stigler, "Stuart Wood and the Marginal Productivity Theory," *Quarterly Journal of Economics* 61 (August 1947): 640–649.

58. John St. George Joyce, *Story of Philadelphia* (n.p.: Harry P. Joseph, 1919), 282.

59. "First Annual Report of the Citizens' Committee of Fifty for a New Philadelphia," January 1, 1892 (n.p., 1892), 1–2.

60. Blankenburg, *Blankenburgs of Philadelphia*, 21–28.

61. William Howe Tolman, *Municipal Reform Movements in the United States* (New York: Fleming H. Revell, 1895).

62. John William Edward, ed., *Who's Who in Finance: A Biographical Dictionary of Contemporary Bankers, Capitalists and Others Engaged in Financial Activities in the United States and Canada* (New York: Joseph and Sefton, 1911), 821–822.

63. James Wolfinger, *Running the Rails: Capital and Labor in the Philadelphia Transit Industry* (Ithaca, NY: Cornell University Press, 2016), 74.

CHAPTER 2

1. Peter McCaffery, *When Bosses Ruled Philadelphia: The Emergence of the Republican Machine, 1867–1933* (University Park: Pennsylvania State University Press, 1993), 82–95, chap. 7; Francis Ryan, *AFSCME's Philadelphia Story: Municipal Workers and Urban Power in the Twentieth Century* (Philadelphia: Temple University Press, 2011), quote on 12.

2. Steffens's article was reprinted in his book *Shame of the Cities* (New York: Sagamore, 1957; originally published by McClure, Phillips, in 1904), quote on 134.

3. McCaffery, *When Bosses Ruled Philadelphia*, 141.

4. Ryan, *AFSCME's Philadelphia Story*, 28–30.

5. William S. Vare, *My Forty Years in Politics* (Philadelphia: Roland Swain, 1933), 86.

6. Vare, *My Forty Years in Politics*, 84–85.

7. Herbert N. Casson, "The Wave of Reform," *Munsey's Magazine*, October 1905, 22.

8. Steffens, *Shame of the Cities*, 160.

9. Daniel Amsterdam, *Roaring Metropolis: Businessmen's Campaigns for a Civic Welfare State* (Philadelphia: University of Pennsylvania Press, 2016), 33.

10. Lloyd M. Abernathy, "Insurgency in Philadelphia, 1905," *Pennsylvania Magazine of History and Biography* 87 (January 1963): 9.

11. Vare, *My Forty Years in Politics*, 89.

12. Vare, *My Forty Years in Politics*, 91–93.

13. Casson, "Wave of Reform," 23.

14. Vare, *My Forty Years in Politics*, 93.

15. Philadelphia Department of Records, "Agency Information: Public Safety, Department of; Public Works, Department of," Record Groups 83, 85, available at www .phila.gov/phils/docs/inventor/graphics/cityagen.htm. Accessed April 13, 2020.

16. Vare, *My Forty Years in Politics*, 95.

17. Quoted in McCaffery, *When Bosses Ruled Philadelphia*, 165.

18. McCaffery, *When Bosses Ruled Philadelphia*, 129.

19. Rosen, *The Philadelphia Fels, 1880–1920* (Madison, NJ: Farleigh Dickinson University Press, 2000), 120; see also Vare, *My Forty Years in Politics*, 102–103.

20. Lincoln Steffens, *Autobiography of Lincoln Steffens* (New York: Harcourt Brace, 1931), 411; see also Abernathy, "Insurgency in Philadelphia," 5–6.

21. McCaffery, *When Bosses Ruled Philadelphia*, 162; Clinton Rogers Woodruff, "The Municipal League of Philadelphia," *American Journal of Sociology* 11 (November 1905): 336–358.

22. Rosen, *Philadelphia Fels*, 118–121.

23. McCaffery, *When Bosses Ruled Philadelphia*, 163.

24. Vare, *My Forty Years in Politics*, 96–97; Abernathy, "Insurgency in Philadelphia," 19.

25. Jerome Bjelopera, *City of Clerks: Office and Sales Workers in Philadelphia, 1870–1920* (Urbana: University of Illinois Press, 2005), chap. 1.

26. John Puckett and Mark Lloyd, *Becoming Penn: The Pragmatic American University, 1950–2000* (Philadelphia: University of Pennsylvania Press, 2015), 6–9.

27. Alissa Falcone, Scott Knowles, Jonson Miller, Tiago Saraiva, and Amy Slaton, "Continuous Reinvention: A History of Engineering Education at Drexel University," in *Building Drexel: The University and Its City, 1891–2016*, ed. Richardson Dilworth and Scott Knowles (Philadelphia: Temple University Press, 2017), 41.

28. Vare, *My Forty Years in Politics*, 105–107.

29. Hindy Lauer Schachter, "Philadelphia's Progressive-Era Bureau of Municipal Research," *Administrative Theory and Praxis* 24 (September 2002): 555–570.

30. Amsterdam, *Roaring Metropolis*, 28–34.

31. James Wolfinger, *Running the Rails: Capital and Labor in the Philadelphia Transit Industry* (Ithaca, NY: Cornell University Press, 2016), 75–78.

32. Vare, *My Forty Years in Politics*, 108–110. On the 1935 law, see Abraham Freedman, "Adventures in Reform," unpublished manuscript dated June 23, 1965 (Abraham L. Freedman papers, 1850–2011, Temple University Urban Archives), 90–91.

33. Wolfinger, *Running the Rails*, 79–84.

34. Vare, *My Forty Years in Politics*, 114–120, quote on 120.

35. Drew Vandecreek, "Unseen Influence: Lucretia Blankenburg and the Rise of Philadelphia Reform Politics in 1911," in *We Have Come to Stay: American Women and Political Parties, 1880–1960*, ed. Melanie Gustafson, Kristie Miller, and Elisabeth Perry (Albuquerque: University of New Mexico Press, 1999), 33.

36. Bonnie Fox, "The Philadelphia Progressives: A Test of the Hofstadter-Hays Thesis," *Pennsylvania History* 34 (October 1967): 372–394; Digby Baltzell, *Puritan Boston and*

Quaker Philadelphia (Boston: Beacon, 1979), 384–385; McCaffery, *When Bosses Ruled Philadelphia*, 166–178.

37. Fox, "Philadelphia Progressives," 393.

38. Lucretia Blankenburg, *Blankenburgs of Philadelphia* (Philadelphia: John C. Winston, 1929), 65.

39. McCaffery, *When Bosses Ruled Philadelphia*, 183–184; Blankenburg, *Blankenburgs of Philadelphia*, chaps. 9–11, Lloyd Abernathy, "Progressivism 1905–1919," in *Philadelphia: A 300-Year History*, ed. Russell Weigley (New York: W. W. Norton, 1982), 555–556.

40. Abernathy, "Progressivism 1905–1919," 556–557.

41. F. W. Coker, "Philadelphia's New Charter," *American Political Science Review* 13 (November 1919): 643–645, quote on 644.

42. Johannes Hoeber, "Philadelphia Carries On," *National Municipal Review* 28 (September 1939): 650.

43. Amsterdam, *Roaring Metropolis*, 87.

44. Arthur Dudden, "The City Embraces 'Normalcy' 1919–1929," in *Philadelphia: A 300-Year History*, ed. Russell Weigley (New York: W. W. Norton, 1982), 584.

45. Ryan, *AFSCME's Philadelphia Story*, 36.

46. Domenic Vitiello, "Machine Building and City Building: Urban Planning and Industrial Restructuring in Philadelphia, 1894–1928," *Journal of Urban History* 34 (March 2008): 399–434.

47. Ryan, *AFSCME's Philadelphia Story*, 36–37, 42.

48. James Wolfinger, *Philadelphia Divided: Race and Politics in the City of Brotherly Love* (Chapel Hill: University of North Carolina Press, 2011), 35, 47–48; Ryan, *AFSCME's Philadelphia Story*, 36.

49. John Rossi, "Philadelphia's Forgotten Mayor: S. Davis Wilson," *Pennsylvania History* 51 (April 1984): 151.

50. Ryan, *AFSCME's Philadelphia Story*, 53.

51. Ryan, *AFSCME's Philadelphia Story*, 47–62.

52. John R. Blackman Jr., "White Denounces Council-Wilson Delay on Budget," *Philadelphia Inquirer* (hereafter *Inquirer*), December 12, 1936, 1, 25, and "Wilson Calls on Earle Again for Budget Aid," *Inquirer*, December 17, 1936, 1, 12. On the wage tax, see also Pennsylvania Economy League, "The Sterling Act: A Brief History," March 1999, available at economyleague.org/providing-insight/reports/1999/01/01/the-sterling-act-a-brief-history. Accessed June 12, 2022.

53. Charles Ellis Jr., "Bill to Drop Tax Levy Offered by Connell," *Inquirer*, December 9, 1938, 1.

54. University of Pittsburgh, University Library System Archives and Special Collections, "Guide to the Pennsylvania Economy League Records, 1925–1985 AIS.1978.06," available at digital.library.pitt.edu/islandora/object/pitt%3AUS-PPiU-ais197806/viewer. Accessed June 12, 2022.

55. "Howard Cooper Johnson," *Inquirer*, January 18, 1938, 13.

56. Blackman, "Wilson Calls on Earle Again for Budget Aid," *Inquirer*, December 17, 1936, 1, 12.

57. John Blackman Jr., "Wilson Urges Year's Budget upon Council," *Inquirer*, December 22, 1936, 1, 9.

58. "City Debt Exceeds Limit $35,700,000, Commission Finds," *Inquirer*, November 16, 1937, 1, 12; "Mayor to Present New Budget Today," *Inquirer*, November 15, 1937, 2.

59. Joseph Miller, "Senate Votes Wide Probe of Phil. Finances," *Inquirer*, January 12, 1937, 1, 9.

60. Hoeber, "Philadelphia Carries On," 647.

61. Margaret Tinkcom, "Depression and War 1929–1946," in *Philadelphia: A 300-Year History*, ed. Russell Weigley (New York: W. W. Norton, 1982), 623–628.

62. Hoeber, "Philadelphia Carries On," 650.

63. Kirk Petshek, *Challenge of Urban Reform: Policies and Programs in Philadelphia* (Philadelphia: Temple University Press, 1973), 16.

64. Gregory Heller, *Ed Bacon: Planning, Politics, and the Building of Modern Philadelphia* (Philadelphia: University of Pennsylvania Press, 2013), 41.

65. Petshek, *Challenge of Urban Reform*, 19.

66. Heller, *Ed Bacon*, 42, 55.

67. Heller, *Ed Bacon*, 44–46.

68. Ryan, *AFSCME's Philadelphia Story*, 105–107; Freedman, "Adventures in Reform," 45–47.

69. John Kromer, *Philadelphia Battlefields: Disruptive Campaigns and Upset Elections in a Changing City* (Philadelphia: Temple University Press, 2020), 36–40.

70. Ryan, *AFSCME's Philadelphia Story*, 112.

71. Joseph Crumlish, *A City Finds Itself: The Philadelphia Home Rule Charter Movement* (Detroit, MI: Wayne State University Press, 1959), 47.

72. Crumlish, *A City Finds Itself*, 21; Ryan, *AFSCME's Philadelphia Story*, 108–109.

73. Quoted in Crumlish, *A City Finds Itself*, 33.

74. Harold Libros, *Hard Core Liberals: A Sociological Analysis of the Philadelphia Americans for Democratic Action* (Cambridge, MA: Schenkman, 1975), 14, 22–23, 73, quote on 56–57.

75. Petshek, *Challenge of Urban Reform*, 49; Ryan, *AFSCME's Philadelphia Story*, 113.

76. Wolfinger, *Philadelphia Divided*, 202–206.

77. Crumlish, *A City Finds Itself*; Petshek, *Challenge of Urban Reform*, 35–36.

78. Crumlish, *A City Finds Itself*, 60.

79. Crumlish, *A City Finds Itself*, 50, 59–66; Peter Binzen and Jonathan Binzen, *Richardson Dilworth: Last of the Bare-Knuckled Aristocrats* (Philadelphia: Camino Books, 2014), chap. 8.

80. Ryan, *AFSCME's Philadelphia Story*, 125–126.

81. Crumlish, *A City Finds Itself*, chap. 7.

82. Margaret Pugh O'Mara, *Cities of Knowledge: Cold War Science and the Search for the Next Silicon Valley* (Princeton, NJ: Princeton University Press, 2005), chaps. 1, 2, 4.

83. Matthew Countryman, *Up South: Civil Rights and Black Power in Philadelphia* (Philadelphia: University of Pennsylvania Press, 2007), 28–32, quote on 29.

84. James Reichley, *Art of Government: Reform and Organization Politics in Philadelphia* (New York: Fund for the Republic, 1959), 61; Guian McKee, *Problem of Jobs: Liberalism, Race, and Deindustrialization in Philadelphia* (Chicago: University of Chicago Press, 2008), 39; Petshek, *Challenge of Urban Reform*, 61; Carolyn Adams, David Bartelt, David Elesh, Ira Goldstein, Nancy Kleniewski, and William Yancey, *Philadelphia: Neighbor-*

hoods, Division, and Conflict in a Postindustrial City (Philadelphia: Temple University Press, 1991), 139.

85. Petshek, *Challenge of Urban Reform*, 30–31.

86. Quoted in Libros, *Hard Core Liberals*, 27.

87. Heller, *Ed Bacon*, 46–53.

88. Marcus Anthony Hunter, *Black Citymakers: How the Philadelphia Negro Changed Urban America* (New York: Oxford University Press, 2013), chap. 4.

89. Heller, *Ed Bacon*, chaps. 4, 5.

90. McKee, *Problem of Jobs*, 38–40; Libros, *Hard Core Liberals*, 21; Heller, *Ed Bacon*, 59–60; *Remaking Center City: A History of the Central Philadelphia Development Corporation* (Philadelphia: Central Philadelphia Development, 2006).

91. Ryan, *AFSCME's Philadelphia Story*, 133.

92. Countryman, *Up South*, 14, 18, 52, 54–55.

93. W. Wilson Goode and Joann Stevens, *In Goode Faith: Philadelphia's First Black Mayor Tells His Story* (Valley Forge, PA: Judson, 1992), 40, 46.

94. Wolfinger, *Philadelphia Divided*, 70, 90–98, 197–202.

95. Ryan, *AFSCME's Philadelphia Story*, 130–133.

96. Wolfinger, *Philadelphia Divided*, 217–233.

97. McKee, *Problem of Jobs*, 39.

98. Timothy Lombardo, *Blue-Collar Conservatism: Frank Rizzo's Philadelphia and Populist Politics* (Philadelphia: University of Pennsylvania Press, 2018), 27.

99. Wolfinger, *Philadelphia Divided*, 231.

100. Kromer, *Philadelphia Battlefields*, 42–45.

101. Ryan, *AFSCME's Philadelphia Story*, 138, 150.

102. Ryan, *AFSCME's Philadelphia Story*, 127; Kromer, *Philadelphia Battlefields*, 222; Petshek, *Challenge of Urban Reform*, 65–67; Libros, *Hard Core Liberals*, 56–57.

103. McKee, *Problem of Jobs*, 73–74; Ryan, *AFSCME's Philadelphia Story*, 123.

104. Countryman, *Up South*, 19–22, 164–171, 230–231, 238–240.

105. Lombardo, *Blue-Collar Conservatism*, 35, 40, 46.

106. Lombardo, *Blue-Collar Conservatism*, chaps. 3, 4.

107. Countryman, *Up South*, 101–117.

108. McKee, *Problem of Jobs*, 229–233, quote on 232.

109. Richard Keiser, *Subordination or Empowerment? African-American Leadership and the Struggle for Urban Political Power* (New York: Oxford University Press, 1997), 101.

110. McKee, *Problem of Jobs*, 250.

111. McKee, *Problem of Jobs*, 99–102.

112. Ryan, *AFSCME's Philadelphia Story*, 155, 169–175.

113. McKee, *Problem of Jobs*, 214–221; Ryan, *AFSCME's Philadelphia Story*, 153.

114. McKee, *Problem of Jobs*, 239–240.

115. Lombardo, *Blue-Collar Conservatism*, 150–151; Ryan, *AFSCME's Philadelphia Story*, 187.

116. Ryan, *AFSCME's Philadelphia Story*, 147; Keiser, *Subordination or Empowerment?* 103–104.

117. Countryman, *Up South*, 310.

118. Keiser, *Subordination or Empowerment?* 106; Thacher Longstreth and Dan Rottenberg, *Main Line WASP* (New York: W. W. Norton, 1990), 260–263.

119. McKee, *Problem of Jobs*, 247.

120. Quoted in Michael Katz, "The Urban 'Underclass' as a Metaphor of Social Transformation," in *The "Underclass" Debate: Views from History*, ed. Michael Katz (Princeton, NJ: Princeton University Press, 1993), 4.

121. Ryan, *AFSCME's Philadelphia Story*, 192–196.

122. Ryan, *AFSCME's Philadelphia Story*, 193–194; Keiser, *Subordination or Empowerment?* 107.

123. Ryan, *AFSCME's Philadelphia Story*, 195; Keiser, *Subordination or Empowerment?* 107–108.

124. Blackwell resigned his council seat to run for mayor but simultaneously ran again for council, won, and was reseated after he lost the mayoral election. See "Candidate Blackwell Quits Council," *Inquirer*, July 31, 1979, B3. Thanks to John Kromer for uncovering this detail.

125. Keiser, *Subordination or Empowerment?* 110.

126. Ryan, *AFSCME's Philadelphia Story*, 212–214.

127. Goode and Stevens, *In Goode Faith*, 149.

128. Arthur Maas, "U.S. Prosecution of State and Local Officials for Political Corruption: Is the Bureaucracy Out of Control in a High-Stakes Operation Involving the Constitutional System?" *Publius* 17 (Summer 1987): 195–230; Ralph Cipriano, *Target: The Senator* (self-pub., 2017), 51–55.

129. Ryan, *AFSCME's Philadelphia Story*, 201–203.

130. Ryan, *AFSCME's Philadelphia Story*, 202.

131. Phyllis Kaniss, *Media and the Mayor's Race: The Failure of Urban Reporting* (Bloomington: Indiana University Press, 1995), 4; Michael Decourcy Hinds, "After Renaissance of the 70's and 80's, Philadelphia Is Struggling to Survive," *New York Times*, June 21, 1990.

132. Dick Polman, "'Black Party' Image Splits Democrats," *Inquirer*, January 14, 1990, A1.

133. Keiser, *Subordination or Empowerment?* 115; Kaniss, *Media and the Mayor's Race*, 33.

134. Polman, "'Black Party' Image Splits Democrats," A1.

135. Kaniss, *Media and the Mayor's Race*, 63, 66.

136. Ryan, *AFSCME's Philadelphia Story*, 218.

137. Kaniss, *Media and the Mayor's Race*, 17.

138. Kaniss, *Media and the Mayor's Race*, 11, 79.

139. Kaniss, *Media and the Mayor's Race*, 15, 93, 124–125, 255–256.

140. Kaniss, *Media and the Mayor's Race*, 31–36, quote on 31.

141. Kaniss, *Media and the Mayor's Race*, 283.

142. Kaniss, *Media and the Mayor's Race*, 256.

143. Keiser, *Subordination or Empowerment?* 125.

144. John Buntin, "25 Years Later, What Happened to 'Reinventing Government?'" *Governing*, August 29, 2016. Available at: www.governing.com/archive/gov-reinventing-government-book.html. Accessed June 12, 2022; See also David Osborne and Ted Gaebler, *Reinventing Government: How the Entrepreneurial Spirit is Transforming the Public Sector* (New York: Penguin, 1993).

145. Stephen McGovern, "Mayoral Leadership and Economic Development Policy: The Case of Ed Rendell's Philadelphia," *Policy and Politics* 25 (1997): 153–172.

146. Ryan, *AFSCME's Philadelphia Story*, 216–230, quote on 221.

147. Amy Rosenberg, "Voters Deliver a Noisy No to City Charter Change," *Inquirer*, May 11, 1994, A1.

148. Kromer, *Philadelphia Battlefields*, 121.

CHAPTER 3

1. *Philadelphia in Focus: A Profile from Census 2000* (Washington, DC: Brookings Institution Center for Urban and Metropolitan Policy, 2003), 17–22, 47, 56–59.

2. Karen Bojar, *Green Shoots of Democracy in the Philadelphia Democratic Party* (Berkeley, CA: She Writes, 2016), chap. 3.

3. Philadelphia City Commissioners, "Voter Registration by Party 1940–2021," available at https://files7.philadelphiavotes.com/department-reports/Historical_Registration_1940-2021G.pdf. Accessed June 12, 2022.

4. Tom Ferrick Jr., "Why Street Won and, More Telling, Why Katz Didn't," *Inquirer*, November 3, 1999, A23.

5. Tom Infield, "A Key Street Ally, a Powerhouse in His Own Right," *Inquirer*, January 15, 2001, A1, A7.

6. See, for instance, Tom Infield, "Local Rivalries Lead to Split on Casey, Rendell," *Inquirer*, May 14, 2002, A1; Larry Platt, "Understanding Bob Brady," *Philadelphia Citizen*, October 12, 2015.

7. Quoted in John Kromer, *Philadelphia Battlefields: Disruptive Campaigns and Upset Elections in a Changing City* (Philadelphia: Temple University Press, 2020), 188. See also Bojar, *Green Shoots of Democracy*, 138.

8. Jacques Steinberg, "In Largest Schools Takeover, State Will Run Philadelphia's," *New York Times*, December 22, 2001, A1; Tricia Nadolny and Angela Couloumbis, "How the Parking Authority Became a Republican Patronage Haven," *Inquirer*, October 2, 2016.

9. Peter Sigal, "Street Celebrates Program to Fight Blight," *Inquirer*, February 25, 2002, B1.

10. Tom Ferrick Jr., "Street Puts on His Election-Day Best," *Inquirer*, February 19, 2003, B1; Michael Nutter, *Mayor: The Best Job in Politics* (Philadelphia: University of Pennsylvania Press, 2018), 43.

11. Anthony Twyman, Nathan Gorenstein, and Emilie Lounsberry, "FBI Raids Three City Agencies, Street Fund-Raiser's Office," *Inquirer*, October 17, 2003, A1.

12. Joel Mathis, "Who Saved John Street's Career?" *Philadelphia Magazine*, March 26, 2015.

13. Emilie Lounsberry and Craig McCoy, "Special Report: Building the Case," *Inquirer*, March 22, 2009, A1; John Shiffman, "Judge Rejects Testing Mariano," *Inquirer*, November 28, 2005, B1.

14. Jeff Shields, "A Big Pay for One-Day Retirement," *Inquirer*, November 17, 2007, A1.

15. Andrew Maykuth, "Poll Finds City Voters Uneasy," *Inquirer*, March 4, 2007, E4.

16. Gwen Shaffer, "Ethical Dilemma," *Philadelphia Weekly*, April 6–12, 2005, 21.

17. Robert D. Putnam, *Bowling Alone: The Collapse and Revival of American Community* (New York: Simon and Schuster, 2000).

18. Marcia Gelbart, "Big Names for the Committee of Seventy," *Inquirer*, November 16, 2005, B1; "Can the Committee of Seventy Clean Up Philadelphia Politics?" *Philadelphia Magazine*, December 17, 2011.

19. Thomas Fitzgerald, "Democrats Seek to Regain Party's Soul," *Inquirer*, June 16, 2005, B1.

20. Thomas Fitzgerald, "Insurgent Democrats Win 64 Seats on Ward Committees," *Inquirer*, May 19, 2006, B1; Thomas Fitzgerald and Marcia Gelbart, "3,248 Cogs Wanting into the Machine," *Inquirer*, March 20, 2006, A1.

21. Thomas Fitzgerald, "Charter Change to Get Mailing by Candidate," *Inquirer*, October 13, 2005, B1.

22. *Philadelphia 2009: The State of the City* (Philadelphia: Pew Charitable Trusts, 2009); *Philadelphia: The State of the City, a 2010 Update* (Philadelphia: Pew Charitable Trusts, 2010).

23. *Philadelphia's Changing Neighborhoods* (Philadelphia: Pew Charitable Trusts, 2016).

24. *Philadelphia 2009*, 9, 14.

25. Inga Saffron, "Two Groups, in Ten Years, Put Urban Design on the City's Agenda," *Inquirer*, September 28, 2012, D1.

26. Patrick Kerkstra, "A Step Toward Revising 46-Year-Old Zoning Code," *Inquirer*, December 7, 2006, B1.

27. Nutter, *Mayor*, 62.

28. Stephen McGovern, "Mobilization on the Waterfront: The Ideological/Cultural Roots of Potential Regime Change in Philadelphia," *Urban Affairs Review* 44 (May 2009): 663–694.

29. "Pew Launches Philadelphia Research Initiative," Pew Charitable Trusts Press Release, November 6, 2008.

30. C. W. Anderson, *Rebuilding the News: Metropolitan Journalism in the Digital Age* (Philadelphia: Temple University Press, 2013), 152–154.

31. William Launder and Russell Adams, "Philadelphia Newspapers Sold Yet Again," *Wall Street Journal*, April 2, 2012; Jeff Gammage, "An Untried Move Draws a Range of Reactions," *Inquirer*, January 13, 2016, A11.

32. *Philadelphia 2013: The State of the City* (Philadelphia: Pew Charitable Trusts, 2013), 36.

33. Thomas Fitzgerald, "Poll Shows Knox with Big Gain," *Inquirer*, March 27, 2007, B5.

34. Thomas Fitzgerald and Michael Matza, "A Different Complexion," *Inquirer*, April 29, 2007, A1.

35. Inga Saffron, "New Zoning Code Reflects a Changing, Growing City," *Inquirer*, August 24, 2012, D1.

36. Patrick Kerkstra, "At-Large Council Challengers Are Intent on Change," *Inquirer*, May 9, 2007, B1.

37. Nutter, *Mayor*, 74–78, quote on 78.

38. Nutter, *Mayor*, 93.

39. Mark Fazlollah and Joseph Tanfani, "It's Who You Know," *Inquirer*, May 4, 2009, A1.

40. Nutter, *Mayor*, 116; Troy Graham, Jeff Shields, and Kristen Graham, "Council Souring on Soda Tax Plan," *Inquirer*, June 15, 2011, A1.

41. Marcia Gelbart and Jeff Shields, "Blue-Collar Workers Endorse Street," *Inquirer*, April 13, 2011, B2.

42. Bob Warner, "After Election Disarray, Philadelphia City Commissioners Try to Regroup," *Inquirer*, November 26, 2012.

43. Jeff Shields, "Allies and Allegiances on New City Council," *Inquirer*, May 23, 2011, A1.

44. *Quiet No More: Philadelphia Confronts the Cost of Employee Benefits* (Philadelphia: Pew Charitable Trusts, 2009); Andrew Maykuth and Claudia Vargas, "Council Nixes Plan to Sell Off the Philadelphia Gas Works," *Inquirer*, October 28, 2014, A1.

45. Nutter, *Mayor*, 152–153.

46. Bojar, *Green Shoots of Democracy*, 154–161.

47. Bojar, *Green Shoots of Democracy*, 170.

48. Simon Van Zuylen-Wood, "Philadelphia Is Ori Feibush's World, We Just Live in It Now," *Philadelphia Magazine*, May 23, 2013.

49. Bojar, *Green Shoots of Democracy*, 162–163.

50. *Philadelphia's Councilmanic Prerogative: How It Works and Why It Matters* (Philadelphia: Pew Charitable Trusts, 2015), quote on 23.

51. Troy Graham, "Developer Sues Philadelphia Councilman," *Inquirer*, June 27, 2014, B1; William Bender, "FBI Said to Be Probing City Public Land Sales," *Inquirer*, May 7, 2016, B1.

52. Ryan Briggs, "Millennial PACs Gain Steam—and Money—in Philadelphia," *Inquirer*, March 4, 2015.

53. Chris Brennan, "Nonprofit Wants to Have Say on Races," *Inquirer*, March 5, 2015, B5; see also Holly Otterbein, "Ali Perelman: New Philly's Old Money," *Philadelphia Magazine*, October 21, 2017.

54. Ernest Owens, "Jamie Gauthier Defeats 27-Year Incumbent Jannie Blackwell in City Council Race," *Philadelphia Magazine*, May 21, 2019.

55. Bojar, *Green Shoots of Democracy*, 162.

56. Malcolm Burnley, "Jon Geeting: The Urbanist," *Philadelphia Magazine*, October 21, 2017. Available at www.phillymag.com/news/2017/10/21/jon-geeting-urbanist/. Accessed June 12, 2022.

57. From the *Inquirer* by Julia Terruso: "Gym Announces Run for Council At-Large," February 10, 2015, B4; "New Faces Backed for Council," March 31, 2015, B2; "Council Candidate 1st to Air TV Spot," April 8, 2015, B2; "At-Large Field Large, Could Make History," May 15, 2015, B1.

58. Larry Platt, "Reformer vs. Progressive," *Philadelphia Citizen*, January 23, 2020. Available at https://thephiladelphiacitizen.org/philadelphia-political-divide/. Accessed June 12, 2022.

59. Ward-level election results come from Jonathan Tannen's blog, available at sixtysixwards.com.

60. Holly Otterbein, "This One Super PAC Raised More Than All the Mayoral Candidates Combined," *Philadelphia Magazine*, May 8, 2015. From the *Inquirer*: Claudia Vargas, "AFL-CIO, PFT and LGBT Leaders Endorse Kenney," March 14, 2015; Robert Moran, "FOP Endorses Kenney in Philly Mayoral Race," March 19, 2015; Chris Brennan, "Kenney Gets Ad Help from Outside Funds," March 25, 2015; Chris Hepp, "Kenney Picks Up Two More Labor Endorsements," April 1, 2015; Chris Hepp, "Evans and African American Leaders Endorse Kenney," April 7, 2015; Chris Hepp, "Inquirer Poll: Kenney Has Big Lead in Mayor's Race," May 14, 2015; Chris Brennan and Julia Terruso, "Kenney Coasts to Victory; 3 Dems to Join High Court," November 4, 2015. My discussion here is a revised version of my essay, "The Making of a Progressive Mayor: James Kenney of Philadelphia," Metropolitics.org, October 17, 2018.

61. Mark Dent, "How Jim Kenney Won His Very First Election," Billypenn.com, October 7, 2015. Available at https://billypenn.com/2015/10/07/how-jim-kenney-won -his-very-first-election-it-had-nothing-to-do-with-me/. Accessed June 12, 2022.

62. Dianna Marder, "Council's Constant Crusader Jim Kenney Is Often a Solo Act," *Inquirer*, January 27, 1997, B1.

63. Julia Terruso, "A Watershed Year Seen for LGBT Political Heft," *Inquirer*, March 14, 2015.

64. Thomas Fitzgerald, "Some See Leftward Big-City Tide," *Inquirer*, May 21, 2015, A1.

65. Julia Terruso, "Five Ways Kenney Would Spend Soda Tax Revenue," *Inquirer*, March 1, 2016. Available at www.inquirer.com/philly/news/politics/20160301_Five _ways_Kenney_would_spend_soda_tax_revenue.html#loaded. Accessed June 12, 2022; Tricia Nadolny and Julia Terruso, "How Kenney and Council Hammered Out the Soda Tax Deal," *Inquirer*, June 12, 2016. Available at www.inquirer.com/philly/news/politics /20160612_How_Kenney_and_Council_hammered_out_the_soda-tax_deal.html. Accessed June 12, 2022.

66. Craig McCoy, Chris Brennan, and Mark Fazlollah, "Cellphones of Labor Leader, Councilman Were Wiretapped," *Inquirer*, June 27, 2017, A1.

67. Monica Marie Zorilla, "Philly's 8-Year Battle to Be a Sanctuary City," Billypenn .com, June 10, 2018.

68. Dave Boyer, "Jim Kenney's Happy Dance over Sanctuary City Ruling 'Disgusting,' White House Says," *Washington Times*, June 7, 2018.

69. Kromer, *Philadelphia Battlefields*, 236.

70. Dave Davies, "Who's Backing Whom in the Philly DA's Race," Whyy.org, May 4, 2017; Thomas Fitzgerald, "Soros Affecting DA Races," *Inquirer*, May 29, 2017, A2.

71. Claudia Vargas and Chris Brennan, "Heralding a New Guard?" *Inquirer*, November 12, 2017, A3.

72. From the *Inquirer*: Holly Otterbein, "Former WHYY Reporter Elizabeth Fiedler Beats Johnny Doc Ally on His Turf," May 15, 2018; Holly Otterbein, "Are Berniecrats about to Take Control of a South Philly Ward?" May 25, 2018; Chris Brennan, "How 'Outsider' Saval Toppled a State Senator," June 14, 2020, B1; Holly Otterbein, "Reclaim Shows How It Advances," July 23, 2018, A1.

73. Thomas Fitzgerald, "New Party Drives a Progressive Agenda," *Inquirer*, June 8, 2014, A2.

74. Anna Orso, "What's the Working Families Party, and How's It Different from Regular Democrats?" *Inquirer*, November 6, 2019. Available at www.inquirer.com/news /philadelphia-working-families-party-explained-progressives-democrats-elections -20191106.html. Accessed June 12, 2022.

75. Juliana Feliciano Reyes, "Low-Wage Worker Unions Are Trying to Flex Their Muscle in Philly's City Council Race," *Inquirer*, September 4, 2019; Chris Brennan, "Meehan Quits as Head of City's Struggling GOP," *Inquirer*, November 10, 2019, B1; Chris Brennan, "State Rep. Martina White Elected New Chair of Philadelphia's Republican City Committee," *Inquirer*, November 12, 2019.

76. Jeremy Roebuck and David Gambacorta, "US Alleges Bribes, Theft," *Inquirer*, January 31, 2019, A1; Ximena Conde, "All You Need to Know about the Bobby Henon and Johnny Doc Convictions," *Inquirer*, November 16, 2021; Maria Pulcinella and Aaron

Moselle, "Philadelphia City Councilmember Bobby Henon Resigns, Two Months after Bribery Conviction," Whyy.org, January 20, 2022.

77. "Unemployment Rate in Philadelphia County/City, PA," Federal Reserve Bank of Saint Louis. Available at fred.stlouisfed.org/series/PAPHIL5URN.

78. Juliana Feliciano Reyes, "Worker Strength," *Inquirer*, January 3, 2021, H1.

79. Laura McCrystal, Oona Goodin-Smith, and Sean Collins Walsh, "How Last Year's Racial Justice Protests Changed Philadelphia Politics," *Inquirer*, June 5, 2021. Available at www.inquirer.com/news/philadelphia-2020-protests-racism-council-kenney-change-20210605.html. Accessed June 12, 2022.

80. Sean Collins Walsh, "Philly Is Set to Create a New Construction Tax and Make Changes to a Big Property Tax Break in a Win for Council President Darrell Clarke," *Inquirer*, December 1, 2020. Available at www.inquirer.com/politics/philadelphia/philadelphia-construction-tax-abatement-city-council-kenney-20201201.html. Accessed June 12, 2022.

81. Danny Hayes and Jennifer L. Lawless, *News Hole: The Demise of Local Journalism and Political Engagement* (New York: Cambridge University Press, 2021).

82. Stephanie Lai and Andrew Seidman, "Voter Turnout Surged across the Philadelphia Region Amid a 'Highly Polarized Electorate,'" *Inquirer*, November 8, 2019.

CONCLUSION

1. Walter Benjamin, *The Arcades Project*, ed. Kevin McLaughlin, trans. Howard Eiland (Cambridge, MA: Harvard University Press, 2002), 119.

INDEX

The letter *f* following a page number denotes a figure.

Richardson Dilworth is Professor of Politics and Head of the Department of Politics at Drexel University. He is the author of *The Urban Origins of Suburban Autonomy*, editor-in-chief of the *Oxford Bibliographies in Urban Studies*, and the editor or coeditor of nine books, including *Social Capital in the City: Community and Civic Life in Philadelphia* (Temple) and, most recently, with Timothy Weaver, *How Ideas Shape Urban Political Development*.